MASTERPIECES OF THE PICTURE GALLERY

Cäcilia Bischoff

Masterpieces of the Picture Gallery

A Brief Guide to the
Kunsthistorisches Museum

edited by Sabine Haag

Volume 5

Media Owner and Editor:
Dr. Sabine Haag
Director-General
Kunsthistorisches
Museum Wien
1010 Vienna,
Burgring 5

Proofreading:
Elisabeth Herrmann
Annette Schäfer
Karin Zeleny

Translation:
Andrea Schellner
John Winbigler

Art Direction:
Stefan Zeisler

Photographic credits:
© Kunsthistorisches
Museum Vienna
Photos:
Stefan Zeisler
Christian Mendez
Alexander Rosoli
Andreas Uldrich
Photo processing:
Michael Aumüller
Thomas Ritter
Sabine Sommer

Graphic design:
Michaela Noll, KHM
Atelier Simma, Vienna

Printed by:
Stiepan Druck, Leobersdorf

Cover illustration:
Cat. No. 85, detail

Back cover illustration:
Cat. No. 27

Illustration on p. 2:
Cat. No. 29, detail

Illustration on p. 6:
Cat. No. 31, detail

Illustration on p. 8:
Cat. No. 52, detail

Illustration on p. 11:
Cat. No. 86, detail

Illustration on p. 13:
Cat. No. 60, detail

Illustration on p. 15:
Cat. No. 67, detail

Illustration on p. 17:
Cat. No. 55, detail

Illustration on p. 19:
Cat. No. 63, detail

Illustration on p. 21:
Cat. No. 83, detail

Illustration on p. 23:
Cat. No. 90, detail

Illustration on p. 24:
Cat. No. 58, detail

Illustration on p. 226:
Cat. No. 10, detail

Short title:
Cäcilia Bischoff
Masterpieces of the
Picture Gallery
(A Brief Guide to the Kunst-
historisches Museum 5)
Vienna 2010

ISBN 978-3-85497-184-9

CONTENTS

FOREWORD

A contemporary account described the young Archduke Ferdinand as being "frightened and distressed" when he peered for the first time into the forty chests that contained the secret treasure of his grandfather, Emperor Maximilian I (1459–1519). He was simply overwhelmed by the magnificence and splendour of the dynastic memorabilia he found: portraits, weapons and armour. And though today's museum visitor, more accustomed to sensation, may find the reaction of the young Habsburg archduke a bit excessive, the collections of the Kunsthistorisches Museum contain such a wealth of masterpieces that the introduction provided by our new series of brief guides is a necessity.

The Gemäldegalerie has the character of a private princely collection, reflecting centuries of European history both in its richness in certain areas of painting as well as its gaps in others. While the Habsburgs had a preference, for example, for Flemish and Venetian painting, their collections contain hardly any English or French works. Particularly well represented are dynastic portraits, some of them – such as the paintings by Velázquez of the young princes and princesses of the Spanish court – are at the same time artworks of the absolutely highest quality. In addition to a number of landscapes and still lifes, many paintings were based on religious, mythological or allegorical themes that are no longer generally familiar and thus require explanation. "Art conveys that which cannot be said. Thus it seems too foolish to try to express it in words. And yet in striving to do so, our understanding can profit in a way that is of benefit to the practice of art." (Goethe, *Maxims and Reflections.*) May this brief guide be an inspiration to the visitor and instructive in the best sense of the word.

Dr. Sabine Haag
Director-General of the Kunsthistorisches Museum

THE HISTORY OF THE GEMÄLDEGALERIE IN THE KUNSTHISTORISCHES MUSEUM

The Kunsthistorisches Museum's Gemäldegalerie (Picture Gallery) had its origin in the former imperial collection and, like other departments of the museum, resulted from the patronage of a series of members of the House of Habsburg. It originated in the 16th and 17th centuries, and by the end of the 18th century – when it was first opened to the public – it was largely in the form we see today. Thus the Vienna Gemäldegalerie is considerably older than other comparable large galleries. It has also preserved its special character as a private princely collection to a greater degree than is the case with other galleries. The special strengths, but also astonishing deficits, of the collection resulted from the distinctive tastes of the individual collectors and their particular preferences, but also from their aversions, as well as the historical and political conditions of their time. The Habsburgs loved things that were complete and mature; thus earlier, developmental phases are not represented. While the collection is almost completely lacking in Italian paintings of the Trecento (1300s) and Quattrocento (1400s), for example, the full flowering of Italian, especially Venetian, painting of the Renaissance as well as Flemish painting of the 16th and 17th centuries is documented with an unusual wealth of masterpieces. All in all, the art of countries that were long dominated by the Habsburgs plays a significant role. There are more works from the southern, Catholic Netherlands, which remained under Spanish Habsburg control, than from Protestant Holland. The most important 17th-century works in the collection came from Northern Italy and the centres of Baroque painting, Bologna, Florence, Naples and Venice. However, the art of countries with which political relations were strained over the centuries is either underrepresented or not present at all. There is an almost complete lack, for example, of French painting from every period.

Under Emperor Maximilian I (1459–1519) the Habsburg art collections began to take shape. The oldest works in the gallery were acquired by him in accordance with his motto that every person is responsible for creating his own posthumous reputation. Maximilian put great store on his family history and commissioned research into the genealogy of the Habsburgs, inventing it when the trail was lost. The list of ancestors was traced back to the legendary heroes of prehistory and to biblical figures, and a series of portraits from the time of Maximilian I has been preserved.

Emperor Rudolf II (1552–1612) was the first Habsburg art collector in the more restricted sense of the word. While his predecessors had already demonstrated an interest in collecting because of their fascination with history, curiosity about the strange and exotic, as well as the pleasure they took in precious materials and the perfect working of them, Emperor Rudolf II was motivated by an additional, decisive criterion: a true love of art that was sometimes a mania. Rudolf had spent the crucial years of his youth at the court of his uncle King Philip II in Spain. There the young man, who was highly talented both intellectually and artistically but introverted and unsociable, was deeply impressed with Philip's collecting activity, ownership and patronage of art and, in particular, with his paintings by Titian and Hieronymus Bosch. Upon his return to Austria, Rudolf moved his residence from Vienna to Prague. By summoning such important scholars as Tycho Brahe, Johannes Kepler and Carolus Clusius to his court and selecting the most precious artworks for his collection, he made the court an international centre of science and art, gaining in the process a sure sense of quality in making further additions. He doggedly pursued artworks until they came into his possession. It is Rudolf II we have to thank for almost all the pictures by Albrecht Dürer (Cat. Nos. 15, 18, 28) and Lucas Cranach (Cat. No. 33) that are found in the Kunsthistorisches Museum today. In Spain he had his ambassador find and purchase 16th-century Italian pictures by Parmigianino (Cat. Nos. 27, 34) and Correggio (Cat. Nos. 31, 32). He inherited famous paintings by Pieter Bruegel the Elder from the estate of his brother Archduke Ernest (1553–1595), who as regent of the Netherlands had either purchased them or received them as gifts (Cat. No. 52, Ill. p. 8). Contemporary paintings are represented by the works of Bartholomäus Spranger (Cat. No. 55), Hans von Aachen (cf. Cat. No. 57), Joseph Heintz, Roelant Savery and others whom Rudolf called to Prague as court painters and who were part of a court workshop that also included sculptors, medallists, goldsmiths and lapidaries. There they created a unique style under the immediate influence of the emperor himself. He played a decisive role in the development of the late Mannerist style of the Prague court, which was based on the work of Correggio and Parmigianino. The artists working in Prague created a refined and elegant but also highly excessive style that was in keeping with Rudolf II's preference for erotic content in the depiction of mostly mythological subjects. In the final years of his life Rudolf II withdrew more and more from conducting the affairs

of state and was finally pushed aside by his ambitious but less-talented brother Matthias (1557–1619), who accused him of being incapable of governing.

After the death of Rudolf, Emperor Matthias, as his successor, moved the court back to Vienna. The Kunstkammer and part of the gallery followed; the part that remained in Prague was plundered and carried off by Swedish troops at the end of the Thirty Years' War (1618–1648). Emperor Ferdinand III (1608–1657) sought to replenish the Prague gallery and commissioned his brother Archduke Leopold Wilhelm (1614–1662) to do so. As regent of the Netherlands he had purchased a number of pictures from the collection of the Duke of Buckingham in 1650; these were sent to Prague and subsequently came to Vienna in the 18th century.

As a collector of paintings, Archduke Leopold Wilhelm made an extremely important contribution to the holdings now in Vienna. It is to his credit that the Gemäldegalerie in the Kunsthistorisches Museum rose to the rank that it enjoys today, in the company of an elite few among the world's great galleries. As the younger brother of the heir to the throne, he was destined for the clergy from early childhood. In his youth he attained a series of high church offices: Bishop of Passau, Strasbourg, Olmütz (now Olomouc, Czech Republic) and Breslau (now Wrocław, Poland) as well as Grand and German Master of the Teutonic Order, a function that had both a religious and a military component. In the latter capacity his brother Emperor Ferdinand III appointed him commander-in-chief of the imperial army in the final phase of the Thirty Years' War. In 1646 he was appointed by his cousin and brother-in-law King Philip IV of Spain to be regent of the Spanish Netherlands, not least because of the military duties involved.

The truly great significance of Archduke Leopold Wilhelm, however, lies in his importance to cultural history. Encouraged by favourable historical conditions, he compiled over the years that followed one of the largest and most important picture galleries of the 17th century (Cat. No. 86, Ill. p. 11). In his decision to focus his collecting activities on paintings, he may have been influenced by the fact that the artistic climate of the Netherlands had always favoured that medium. Within a period of nine years he built a collection of around

1400 first-rate pictures, at the same time purchasing tapestries, small bronze statuary and drawings as well. Around the middle of the 17th century, a number of large art collections were broken up in the turmoil of the English Civil War. Leopold Wilhelm's initial military and political success in the Netherlands made him an interesting potential buyer. Thus he was offered the art collection of the Duke of Buckingham, who had been assassinated in 1628. The collection had been taken to the Netherlands to protect it and was threatened with confiscation by the English Parliament. Leopold Wilhelm purchased it in the name and at the expense of his brother Emperor Ferdinand III.

Soon after this first major involvement in the Netherlands art market, Leopold Wilhelm purchased for himself the paintings of the Duke of Hamilton, who had been executed in England in 1649. This laid the foundation for his collection of 16th-century Italian paintings. One of the special strengths of the Vienna gallery today, the large number of Venetian paintings, resulted almost entirely from this purchase (Cat. Nos. 40, 73). In his preference for Venetian painting over the works of other Italian schools, the archduke shared a taste that had been established by the Spanish Habsburgs Charles V and Philip II.

Alongside the Italian paintings, the much more numerous holdings of Netherlands works in Leopold Wilhelm's collection deserve mention. He had purchased a small but select group of Early Netherlandish pictures of the 15th century from dealers in Antwerp (Cat. Nos. 1, 2, 4, 7), but most of the Netherlandish pictures are by contemporary Flemish painters, most of them working in the same city (Cat. Nos. 66, 69, 79). The completeness of the list of important artists' names in his collection is evidence of the archduke's sense of purpose in building his collection. In a modern manner he sought to provide an overall perspective of the development of art, also purchasing works by young and yet-unknown artists. At the same time, his personal taste is clear: he preferred small, perfect cabinet pictures, expertly executed flower paintings (Cat. No. 60, Ill. p. 13) and the works of the Netherlandish "fine painters".

In selecting these acquisitions, the archduke's court painters served as his advisors, first Jan van den Hoecke, later David Teniers the Younger and Jan Anthonis van der Baren. In addition, Teniers documented Leopold Wilhelm's

collection in a series of views of his gallery in which the archduke is depicted with various members of his court surrounded by the paintings of his collection. Several years later, Teniers was entrusted by the archduke with a second important task: the publication of the *Theatrum Pictorium,* an illustrated catalogue of the gallery. The first part with 244 etchings of Italian paintings appeared in Brussels in 1660, at a time when the gallery had already been moved to Vienna.

Because Leopold Wilhelm was unable to continue the series of military successes he achieved between 1647 and 1653 against France, he gave up the regency of the southern Netherlands, and on 9 May 1656, he left Brussels and travelled to Austria. It was only in the following year that the collection was transported to Vienna and efforts were begun to exhibit it in the Stallburg, a section of Vienna's Hofburg Palace that had been built in the 16th century. In 1659 a complete inventory was taken, and this remains our most important source in determining the exact size and composition of the collection. Archduke Leopold Wilhelm died in 1662, having named his nephew, later Emperor Leopold I (1640–1705), as his heir. The gallery was integrated into the imperial collection where it became the principal component. Although its size was reduced by half over the centuries, it remains alive today as an important element in the Gemäldegalerie of the Kunsthistorisches Museum in Vienna.

Under Leopold I the Habsburg art collection grew to gigantic size, including as it did the ancestral holdings that he had inherited from his father, Emperor Ferdinand III, augmented by the collection of Archduke Leopold Wilhelm and finally by his own acquisitions. For the most part the latter were coincidental inheritances from the Tirolean line of the Habsburgs rather than planned acquisitions. In addition, the close familial ties to the grand dukes of Tuscany from the House of Medici added numerous paintings by the Florentine school of 17th-century painters. But Spanish relatives also sent family portraits to Vienna, including the famous series of paintings of Spanish princesses by Diego Velázquez.

The son of Leopold I, Charles VI (1685–1740), united most of the imperial art collections in Vienna, but the collection of Archduke Ferdinand II at Ambras Castle near Innsbruck remained there as a separate collection into the 19th century. The Picture Gallery was newly exhibited in Vienna's Stallburg, where Leopold

Wilhelm's gallery had already been established (Cat. No. 67, Ill. p. 15). This new hanging according to late-Baroque, decorative principles was completed in 1728. The walls were covered with richly ornamented and gilt decoration, and the pictures were hung in groups in the interstices. More attention was paid to the overall impression than to the individual object. Grouped symmetrically, with large and small pictures creating a decorative pattern on the respective wall, the paintings were hung without regard to their art-historical context, and the format of individual pictures was altered by cutting them down or adding to them. A magnificent, painted inventory in three volumes by Ferdinand Storffer (actually Astorffer), which depicts the gallery walls in detail, as well as publications of engravings provide excellent documentation of the collection's appearance at the time.

Only fifty years later, the exhibition scheme was already considered anachronistic. The painter Joseph Rosa, who was appointed director of the Gemäldegalerie in 1772, planned to rehang the gallery completely. He reviewed the painting collections that had remained at the imperial palaces in Prague, Pressburg (now Bratislava, Slovakia), Innsbruck and Graz and had the paintings brought to Vienna, where he compiled the first complete inventory of the gallery. In 1775 Rosa was sent to Antwerp in what was still the Austrian Netherlands in order to acquire paintings for the Vienna gallery, in particular some by Peter Paul Rubens and Anthony van Dyck. These works had been the property of the Jesuit order, which had been disbanded a few years earlier. Among the paintings purchased for the Vienna gallery at that time were the large altar-pieces from the Jesuit Church in Antwerp, *The Miracles of St. Ignatius of Loyola, The Miracles of St. Francis Xavier* (Cat. Nos. 62 and 63, Ill. p. 19) and *The Assumption of the Virgin* as well as the *Triptych of St. Ildefonso* by Rubens (Cat. No. 70). Some of these new acquisitions were so large that there was simply no space big enough for them in the low rooms of the Stallburg.

Emperor Joseph II (1741–1790) decided to make the Belvedere Palace the new home of the imperial gallery. Built in 1721 as a summer residence for Prince Eugene, it had been purchased from his estate by Empress Maria Theresa in 1752. A short time later, Christian von Mechel, an engraver, publisher and art connoisseur from Basel, was commissioned to reorganise and rehang the gallery.

For the first time the paintings were organised from an art-historical standpoint: there were two departments, one with Italian and the other with Netherlandish and German paintings. Within each department, the pictures were organised according to chronology and local schools, and this dichotomy in the Gemäldegalerie of the Kunsthistorisches Museum has been preserved down to the present day. In the spirit of the Enlightenment, the gallery was opened to the general public "as a large, public collection, intended more to instruct than simply to provide temporary enjoyment", as stated in the introduction to Christian Mechel's first printed catalogue (1783), which appeared at the time.

The gallery was now intended to present as complete a history of painting as possible. Because there were far fewer Netherlandish than Flemish paintings, an effort was made in the early 19th century to acquire art from the northern Netherlands (Cat. No. 83, Ill. p. 21). In order to round out the gallery's collection, the two brothers Emperor Francis II (I) (1768–1835) and Grand Duke Ferdinand III of Tuscany (1769–1824) decided to exchange pictures between the galleries in Vienna and Florence. Vienna mostly received Florentine paintings of the 16th and 17th centuries but lost masterpieces by Bellini, Titian and Dürer.

The conquest of Vienna by Napoleon's troops (1809) brought drastic change to the gallery. It had not been possible to move the pictures to safety in time, the gallery's holdings were confiscated, and much was taken to Paris. It was not until 1815, following the final peace settlement at the Congress of Vienna, that the collection returned to the Austrian capital.

Most of the important galleries were created in the late 18th and 19th centuries, and during the 19th century many new museums were founded. Collecting activity at the Vienna gallery, however, came to an almost complete halt during this period. The only major additions were those made to the collection of contemporary paintings. In the 19th century the most important accomplishment was the unification of the various imperial art collections, which had formerly been separated in both a physical and organizational sense. They were brought together in a building especially erected for the purpose, the Kunsthistorisches Museum. With the new wing of the Hofburg Palace and the buildings of

the Court Stables – which reopened in 2001 as the MuseumsQuartier – two museum buildings, one each for the art-history and natural-history collections, were to form the so-called Imperial Forum enclosing a large square. The original planning work was done by the great German architect Gottfried Semper (1803–1879), who in 1849 had designed the Dresden gallery, and by Carl von Hasenauer (1833–1894). Construction began in 1871, and the exterior of both museums was complete by 1880. It took another ten years to finish the rich interior and furnishings of the Kunsthistorisches Museum, which finally opened in 1891. Among the great museum buildings of Central Europe, it was the last to be completed and is also the largest and most lavishly decorated. After the end of the First World War and the collapse of the Austro-Hungarian Empire (1918), the imperial collections became the property of the new Republic of Austria. The Österreichische Staatsgalerie (Austrian State Gallery), which had been founded in the final years of the 19th century, received the collection of 19th-century Austrian paintings, while the Gemäldegalerie increasingly turned to new collecting areas – especially Austrian and German painting of the 15th as well as Italian painting of the 18th century. Under the leadership of Gustav Glück, new collecting activity began during a period of extremely difficult economic conditions. Among his acquisitions was the *Portrait of a Young Venetian Woman* by Albrecht Dürer (Cat. No. 11). After 1945 the collection was again restructured, and parts of it were moved; the Österreichische Galerie became a "national gallery" in image with responsibility for the entire field of Austrian painting. In 1986 it also became responsible for all 19th-century works created outside Austria.

Like all the great princely collections of paintings in Europe, the Kunsthistorisches Museum's Gemäldegalerie is now practically complete; new acquisitions are made only to round off and put the final touches to the existing collection, not to change it in any fundamental manner. Nevertheless, the collection is not "dead"; its life is constantly being renewed by its visitors, who are always bringing new insight to bear, even on works they may have often seen, giving them new life.

Dr. Karl Schütz
Director of the Gemäldegalerie

CATALOGUE

1 KARDINAL NICCOLÒ ALBERGATI (?)

JAN VAN EYCK
(Maaseick, ca. 1380/90 –
Bruges, 1441)
1438
Wood, 34.1 x 27.3 cm
Inv. No. 975

In 1435 Jan van Eyck travelled from Bruges to Arras at the request of Duke Philip the Good of Burgundy, whose privileged court painter he had been for the past ten years. During a peace congress that was seeking to bring an end to decades of enmity between France and Burgundy, van Eyck painted portraits of some of those in attendance, among them, most likely, Cardinal Niccolò Albergati, who in his position as nuncio was one the most important participants in the negotiations. In Arras, van Eyck created a silverpoint drawing (Dresden, Staatliche Kunstsammlungen, Kupferstichkabinett), which most probably depicts the cardinal. Here the Flemish painter not only captured the physiognomy of the aged cleric but in his notes also specified the coloration. The painting was conceived several years after the encounter in Arras. Some experts have expressed conflicting opinions regarding the identity of the subject. Beginning in the 7th century a specific hairstyle was obligatory for all Christian clergyman: the so-called tonsure, in which a small round area at the crown of the head was shaved or shorn. The subject of the portrait, however, does not have this feature. His attire is equally unusual: fur trim is not traditionally part of a cardinal's vestment.

With consistent realism and accuracy down to the smallest detail, van Eyck depicts the distinctive and somewhat coarse features of the cleric. The monochrome, dark background focuses the viewer's concentration on the subject's face. Contrary to a myth in art history, van Eyck did not invent oil painting, i.e., the use of oil-soluble resins as binders. However, with the new technique he did introduce fine painting, which had already reached its full flowering in book illumination, to the larger format of the panel painting. The thinly varnished application of pigments created a previously unknown lustre and allowed van Eyck to achieve a high level of definition on extremely varied surfaces and to render exceptionally fine details.

2 TRIPTYCH: THE CRUCIFIXION

ROGIER VAN DER WEYDEN
(Tournai, 1399/1400 –
Brussels, 1464)
Ca. 1443/45
Wood,
centre panel: 96 x 69 cm,
side wings: 101 x 35 cm each
Inv. No. 901

Along with Jan van Eyck, Rogier van der Weyden dominated Netherlandish painting in Brussels in the first half of the 15th century, working both for the Burgundian court as well as for the urban patriciate. We know that in 1450 he undertook a pilgrimage to Rome. The Vienna painting, however, was created before this journey to Italy, which in the following century was to set the standard for artistic training. Today this Crucifixion scene is spread across a winged altar, but it was probably originally a single panel, with the "frame" only painted onto it. Not long after it was created, however, the work was sawn into three parts, making the portraits of St. Mary Magdalene and St. Veronica wings of a triptych. Given its original condition, it makes van der Weyden's artistic innovation even more significant: for the first time he unites all of the participants – the Crucifixion group, saints and the donors – in front of a continuous landscape, in which an idealised Jerusalem appears on the horizon. The realism of such a unified space had never been attempted in earlier works. Unknown today, the patrons are separated only by a conspicuous fissure in the ground from the central subject of religious contemplation, a concept that was so progressive that it was initially attenuated in the paintings of the period that followed. For a long time afterwards, the donors, accompanied by their patron saints, were depicted on the wings of the altar. And there is a second innovation as well: Christ's loincloth, which seems to be blowing in the breeze. It became a motif frequently employed in Netherlandish and German painting.

3 ST. SEBASTIAN

ANDREA MANTEGNA
(Isola di Carturo, 1430/31 –
Mantua, 1506)
Ca. 1457/59
Wood, 68 x 30 cm
Inv. No. 301

According to legend, the emperor Diocletian recruited Sebastian in 303 AD to be an officer in the imperial bodyguard, but Sebastian continued to defend his Christian faith. The *Legenda Aurea* (1265/66; *Golden Legend*) also tells about the impressive healing of Cromatius: the severely ill prefect had summoned Sebastian and Polycarpus, a Christian priest. They immediately baptised him and he was miraculously healed. To further support this new faith, Sebastian destroyed hundreds of idols in Cromatius's house. When Diocletian heard of it, he ordered the execution of Sebastian, who miraculously survived the archers' attempt to kill him with arrows. Diocletian then ordered that he be beaten to death with clubs. The saint has been venerated since the 7th century for his ability to turn away the plague. In the early 15th century, it became usual to depict Sebastian – both north and south of the Alps – as a naked youth clad only in a loincloth.

Mantegna, who was the most important Upper Italian painter of the Quattrocento, became court painter to the Gonzaga in Mantua in 1459. This is the first of his Sebastians and was probably painted a short time earlier in Padua. It documents his intensive study of ancient architecture and sculpture. The ability to depict a space in exact perspective was an accomplishment of the early Florentine Renaissance. The realism in this depiction of Sebastian's injuries and pain had seldom been found in such a clear and unmistakable form before. Perhaps the rider in the clouds at the above left is a reference to the transitoriness of human life. The archers have left the scene; three of them can be seen in the background at the left as they climb a curving path. Fragments of ancient sculpture at the left on the tile floor of a ruined Roman basilica are perhaps a reference to Cromatius. Like the architectural setting, they testify in particular to a reawakened knowledge of ancient culture.

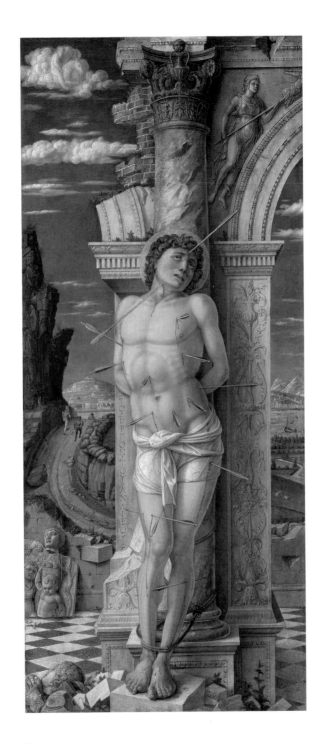

4 THE FALL OF MAN AND THE LAMENTATION

HUGO VAN DER GOES
(Ghent, ca. 1440 – Roode
Klooster near Brussels, 1482)
Ca. 1470/75
Wood, 32.3 x 21.9 cm and
34.4 x 22.8 cm, respectively
Inv. Nos. 5822 A and 945

As contrasting pairs, the Fall and the Redemption of Man, death and life, a paradise flooded with light and a dark overcast horizon, find their formal counterpart in this stylistic and compositional realisation of the theme. The delicate and sharply contoured bodies of the first two human beings are quite different from the figures in the Lamentation, which are interpreted in a painterly fashion and set restlessly into the scene in a continuation of the tradition of Rogier van der Weyden's expressive painting (cf. Cat. No. 2). This has led to the supposition that the two panels were painted at different points in time, rather far apart from one another. Goes, in his striking rendition of the "tempter" with the head of a woman, body of a salamander and feet of an aquatic bird, was falling back on an existing tradition that was occasionally found in Netherlandish (book) paintings.

The work is mentioned in 1659 in the inventory of the collection of Archduke Leopold Wilhelm but attributed in error to Jan van Eyck. Later all knowledge was lost that the two panels of the diptych, which had meanwhile been separated, belonged together. The former outside panel has also been preserved (KHM, GG, Inv. No. 5822 B). They were not presented together again until 1884 and 1887, by that time attributed to van der Goes.

Initially, Hugo van der Goes worked primarily in Ghent. His involvement in the decorations for the wedding of Charles the Bold of Burgundy to Margaret of York in Bruges in 1468, however, brought him more widespread fame, awakening the interest of the archduke and later emperor Maximilian. The latter visited the painter in 1477 during a stay in Ghent and Brussels on the occasion of his marriage to Mary of Burgundy. By then, Goes, who was already suffering from depression, had entered the quiet seclusion of a monastery.

5 MADONNA WITH THE SAINTS NICHOLAS OF BARI, ANASTASIA, URSULA AND DOMINIC

ANTONELLO DA MESSINA
(Messina, ca. 1430 –
Messina, 1479)
Ca. 1475/76
Wood, 115 x 133 cm
Inv. No. 2574

We know that a patrician by the name of Pietro Bon commissioned this altarpiece in 1475 for the Venetian Church of San Cassiano. While the painting was still being completed, the proud donor described it as a work that promised to be "one of the most splendid in the whole of Italy and beyond". The painting was praised in the art literature of the years that followed, but in the 17th century it was cut (for unknown reasons) into five individual panels, which came to the Brussels collection of Archduke Leopold Wilhelm, but only these three were preserved. Only in the early 20th century was it again recognised that the three panels belonged together and that they were the work of Antonello da Messina. The identity of the missing saints has been reconstructed with the help of works by David Teniers (cf. Cat. No. 81), who made miniatures of many of the paintings in the archduke's collection: Cecilia and George were once seen on the left, next to Magdalene and Nicholas; Helen and Sebastian stood on the right behind Ursula and Dominic – the trace of a profile can still be seen at the right edge. The space below Mary's throne was probably occupied by music-making angels. Finally, the uniformly illuminated group was probably originally set into niche architecture seen from a central perspective. Thus the artist created a *sacra conversazione*, a grouping of saints around the Madonna and Child, which had been used by artists for a long time.

When Antonello da Messina received this commission, he had just returned to Venice from Sicily. He had become familiar with Netherlandish painting in Naples, perhaps even earlier in Bruges. There had been efforts before him to introduce the northern technique of oil painting to Upper Italy, but Antonello da Messina's contribution was important. By comparison with tempera painting, the new technique made it possible to depict the material qualities of things in a more differentiated manner and to create more subtle lighting effects.

6 THE HOLY FAMILY

MARTIN SCHONGAUER
(Colmar, ca. 1435/50 –
Breisach, 1491)
Ca. 1480/90
Wood, 26 x 17 cm
Inv. No. 843

The journey of the young Albrecht Dürer to Breisach, where Schongauer had settled in 1488, became legendary. Embarking on his journey from Basel, the Nuremberg painter intended to meet his admired colleague but reached the village of Breisach too late: Schongauer had died a year earlier, probably of the plague.

Schongauer's date of birth is disputed: his existence is first documented in 1465 when he was registered for one semester at the University of Leipzig. Giorgio Vasari, the great artists' biographer of the 16th century, praised Schongauer's copperplate engravings, which established his reputation by virtue of their technical precision and inexhaustible variety of forms and motifs. In his paintings Schongauer combined the qualities of his drawings with a Netherlandish style of coloration adopted from Jan van Eyck and Rogier van der Weyden. This small devotional picture is one of only seven paintings clearly attributable to the southern German artist, who began his career in his father's goldsmith's workshop.

The intimate scene depicts the Virgin Mary and the infant Jesus lost in the deep contemplation of a grape. This symbolic reference to the blood of Christ is seen once more in the basket filled with red grapes at the bottom right. In the small niche above is a water vessel, a simple Madonna attribute symbolising the purity of water. The emphasis on Joseph as the bread-winner of the family – depicted here with a sheaf of wheat, which simultaneously alludes to Christ's redemption – gained importance in the 15th century. Joseph watches the idyllic scene from the back of the Bethlehem stable and thus reflects the role of the devout viewer.

7 LEGEND OF THE RELICS OF ST. JOHN THE BAPTIST

GEERTGEN TOT SINT JANS
(Leiden?, 1460/65 –
Haarlem, after 1490)
After 1484
Wood, 172 x 139 cm
Inv. No. 993

The present painting is the remnant of what was once a remarkably large altarpiece, created by Geertgen on a commission from the Haarlem Order of St. John of Jerusalem. He was probably an "inhabitant" of the order – the Sint-Jans-Heren (thus the painter's name) gave him shelter without requiring him to join. During the siege of the city by the Spanish in 1573 the triptych was destroyed. While the right wing remained, the front and back were separated (back: *The Lamentation of Christ*; KHM, GG, Inv. No. 991). The commission was prompted by a diplomatic gift of Sultan Bayezid to the order, then called the Knights of Rhodes, in 1484: he bequeathed the order relics (arm and fingers) of St. John the Baptist from Jerusalem.

Herodias had persuaded her daughter, Salome, to demand the head of John the Baptist from her stepfather, Herod Antipas, in return for her dancing at his birthday feast (Matt. 14:6–12; Mark 6:21–28). Geertgen depicts the burial of St. John in the background, while Herodias is seen hiding his head in the palace garden, stretched out behind the tomb. According to medieval legend, Emperor Julian the Apostate (361 – 363 AD), who appears with his entourage at the front of the painting, later ordered the burning of St. John's corpse. But monks who happened to be present prevented the complete destruction of the relics. The circumstances surrounding the commissioning of this altarpiece altered the legend at this point, however: here a delegation from the order is seen standing at the open tomb; at the upper right they are taking the rescued relics to Jerusalem.

The combination of various successive episodes in a single painting is in keeping with older tradition; in his composition Geertgen arranges them behind and on top of each other. In comparison to other southern Netherlandish and Flemish works, the most distinguishing feature is the lack of distance to the viewer, which includes the figures in the background. Clear lighting and strong coloration leave no detail unexplained.

With the group of figures standing at the open tomb, Geertgen also created the first group portrait in Netherlandish painting. It is a special local type, which is also found in later works, such as Rembrandt's famous *Night Watch*.

8 SMALL TRIPTYCH OF ST. JOHN THE BAPTIST

HANS MEMLING
(Seligenstadt, ca. 1435/40 –
Bruges, 1494)
Ca. 1485/90
Wood,
centre panel: 69 x 47 cm,
side wings: 69.3 x 17.3 cm
each
Inv. Nos. 939, 943 a and b

After a stay in Cologne (where he possibly studied under Stephan Lochner), Memling probably joined the workshop of Rogier van der Weyden in Brussels. Following the master's death in 1465, the younger artist moved to Bruges, where he assumed a leading position among the painters there. The solemn tranquillity of his compositions and the soft outlines, as compared to the works of van der Weyden, lend his religious paintings an often charming ambience. As in earlier works, Memling adopted from the artistic repertoire of Jan van Eyck the motif of the Madonna sitting enthroned under a brocade-covered canopy. However, it was probably his idea to place the group in front of columned architecture opening into a landscape.

The Vienna triptych also includes a detail that was inspired by Italian models and was an innovation in Netherlandish painting: Memling integrates "living" portal sculpture in the central of the three arches. Putti at play span richly decorated festoons from both sides of the arch to its vertex. In addition, the edges of the arch depict the sacrifice of Isaac and the daughter of Jephthah on the left and right, respectively. Both scenes are prefigurations of the Crucifixion, events from the Old Testament paving the way for the New.

The figure of the client who originally commissioned the triptych (possibly Jan Crabe, abbot of the Flemish monastery Ter Duinen in Koksijde, † 1485) was apparently replaced by the present, unknown donor several years after the work was created. The former side wings of the small folding altar have been preserved (KHM, GG, Inv. Nos. 994 a and b). They present nude depictions of Adam and Eve, also based on the models of Jan van Eyck.

40

9   THE CRUCIFIXION

LUCAS CRANACH THE ELDER
(Kronach, 1472 –
Weimar, 1553)
Ca. 1500
Wood, 58.5 x 45 cm
Inv. No. 6905

Born in the Frankish city of Kronach, Lucas Cranach was summoned to the court of the Saxon elector in Wittenberg in 1504. His date of birth is generally accepted as 1472, but little is known about his biography and work before his appointment 33 years later as court painter in Wittenberg. He is known to have lived in Vienna as early as 1498, where he was in close contact with Humanists at the university, and these connections may have led to his appointment by the elector Frederick the Wise.

First mentioned in the inventory of Vienna's Abbey of the Scots in 1800, the present *Crucifixion* is the first work that can be clearly attributed to the painter. It is conspicuously different from the works he was to create in Wittenberg only a short time later. Here Cranach sticks to a symmetrically arranged Crucifixion group of the traditional type but "dramatises" the scene by creating formal equality between the human figures and their vegetal surroundings.

Nervous brush strokes are juxtaposed to soft outlines; detailed coloration and balanced lighting create a unified impression in the final image. In its delineation, the unusually clear depiction of the tortured body of Christ corresponds with parts of the vegetation in the background. Because of these characteristics, the present painting is regarded as a forerunner of the so-called Danube school of painting, of which Albrecht Altdorfer (Cat. No. 24) became the most prominent exponent. The painting probably also includes a reference to Cranach's earlier stay in Poland: it has recently been suggested that the attire of the group at the right is that of Polish-Lithuanian horsemen.

GIORGIO DA CASTELFRANCO,
CALLED GIORGIONE
(Castelfranco Veneto,
ca. 1477 – Venice, 1510)
Ca. 1504
Canvas, 123.8 x 144.5 cm
Inv. No. 111

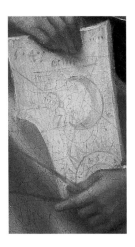

In his *Notizia d'opere del disegno* (1523–1541) the Venetian art collector Marcantonio Michiel draws up an inventory of eleven private picture collections: "[…] The oil painting with the three philosophers set against a landscape […] with this truly wonderfully painted rock […]." According to his account, this large work was in the possession of the Venetian merchant Taddeo Contarini in 1525. At the end of the 16th century it was acquired by Bartolomeo della Nave, also a merchant and collector. It first came to England after his death and in the mid-17th century was finally purchased for Archduke Leopold Wilhelm's Brussels collection. There it was cut down by 17.5 cm on the left side, so that the depiction of nature which had originally formed a remarkably large part of the painting was considerably reduced and the slight asymmetry often found in Giorgione's compositions was somewhat lessened.

Despite the early and rather general identification of the depicted figures as "philosophers", there have been numerous other interpretations, none of which, however, has succeeded in explaining all the details. Are the three figures the Three Kings, astronomers, representatives of three religions or the rival exponents of painting, philosophy and astrology? Recently, Pythagoras and his two teachers, Thales und Pherecydes, have also been mentioned. The features usually cited in these varied interpretations are the compasses and the square, which the seated and youngest of the three men is holding in his hands and which are seen as attributes of a painter (?), the varied origins of the three figures' attire and the astronomical writings held on the far right by the eldest of the three men.

Undisputed is the artistic importance of this major work of Venetian painting. The intensity of colour and light, the juxtaposition of sharply contoured surfaces and blurred outlines *(sfumato)* in connection with the probably intended cryptic message create a mysterious mood and atmosphere, particularly because of the ambiguity of the portrayal.

11   PORTRAIT OF A YOUNG VENETIAN WOMAN

ALBRECHT DÜRER
(Nuremberg, 1471 –
Nuremberg, 1528)
1505
Wood, 32.5 x 24.5 cm
Inv. No. 6440

This honest, close-up view of a gentle face is in keeping with Venetian portraits of the time. The sandy hair of the unknown woman is held at the back of the head by a shining golden net, the prevailing fashion in Venice. Dürer has used carefully distributed highlights to emphasise the curly hair falling to either side of the face; it has a formal counterpart in the fine ribbons of her dress. The fact that Dürer left the preparatory underdrawing of the ribbon on the left has led to the assumption that the picture is unfinished, but technical analysis of the entire surface of the painting speaks against it. It makes sense from a compositional point of view: the colour of the one ribbon matches the woman's hair, while the other picks up the monochrome tone of the background and is also found in the young woman's dark eyes.

Dürer arrived in Venice in the late autumn of 1505. This portrait is believed to be the first work he painted there. In addition to his adoption of the typical composition of Venetian portraits, the refreshing influence of Dürer's new environment is also seen in his suppression of details in favour of a comprehensive view of the whole. Compared with works that he painted in the north, Dürer altered the character of the light, which appears gentle and unifying instead of brightly illuminating every contour. Anticipating his return to the north in January 1507, Dürer wrote to his friend Willibald Pirckheimer a lament that has become famous: "O wy wirt mich noch der sunnen friren. Hy pin jch ein her, doheim ein schmarotzer." ("Oh, how shall I freeze after this sun! Here I am a gentleman, at home a parasite.")

Until it was purchased by the Kunsthistorisches Museum in 1923, the work was in the possession of a Lithuanian collector and unnoticed by the art world.

12 MADONNA IN THE MEADOW

RAPHAEL (RAFFAELLO SANTI)
(Urbino, 1483 –
Rome, 1520)
1505 or 1506
Wood, 113 x 88.5 cm
Inv. No. 175

In 1504 the young Raphael came from Perugia to Florence, where Leonardo da Vinci and Michelangelo dominated artistic life. Especially under the influence of Leonardo's compositions, the newcomer created a series of Madonna depictions. Particularly in Florence, the Madonna image had experienced a change in function: it was no longer mainly a religious item for practical use, but primarily an exquisite expression of artistic achievement. Raphael gave the *Madonna in the Meadow* to his Florentine patron Taddeo Taddi as a gift; in 1662 it was acquired at its place of origin by Archduke Ferdinand Karl of Tirol.

In keeping with the Sienese type of the *Madonna Humilitatis* the Virgin Mary is sitting on an elevation on the ground. Supporting the infant Jesus with both hands, she looks at little John the Baptist. The encounter of the two children has been mentioned in Tuscan devotional literature since the late 13th century. The cross is simultaneously a toy, an attribute of John the Baptist and a Passion symbol. The latter is also true of the conspicuously positioned poppy on the right. In the present painting, which was created at the beginning of his series of full-length Madonna depictions, Raphael decided on a strictly geometrical structure: the group is incorporated in an equilateral triangle. However, within the seemingly rigid structure, a lively scene unfolds. Parallel and opposing movements and glances blend with the landscape in the background to create a composition that is in keeping with the demands of the High Renaissance for perfect balance and harmony.

13 YOUNG WOMAN ("LAURA")

GIORGIO DA CASTELFRANCO,
CALLED GIORGIONE
(Castelfranco Veneto,
ca. 1477 – Venice, 1510)
1506
Canvas on wood,
41 x 33.5 cm
Inv. No. 31

"[…] on 1 June 1506, this was made by the hand of the master Giorgio da Castelfranco, the colleague of master Vincenzo Catena, at the instigation of Mr. Giacomo." This inscription on the back of the painting, translated here from the Italian, gives us one of our few fixed points in the life and work of Giorgione (cf. Cat. No. 10).

The half-length portrait depicts a young woman in a fur-trimmed red cloak. Muted colouring and the fine Venetian shading of *sfumato,* actually adopted from Leonardo, combine with the sensual character of the subject to produce a convincing unity. A white veil is wrapped across the young woman's coiffured hair and falls in a gentle arc over the soft skin of her upper body. Right behind her, set off against a dark background, rises a vigorous laurel-tree (Italian: *lauro*). It may be intended as a coded reference to the subject's name but could also be an attribute of poetry, a symbol of the wish for fidelity in marriage or a reference to Daphne – all of these interpretations are possible. And yet another possibility has also been discussed, one that has to do with the ambiguity in the position of her hand and the character of her clothing. The winter clothing of wealthy Venetian courtesans was usually a beautiful garment lined with fur. Is the young woman closing her cloak or is she about to let it fall? In any case, with this portrait Giorgione created a prototype for later depictions of courtesans and sweethearts in Venetian painting (Cat. Nos. 19, 21, 35, 73).

14   GIPSY MADONNA

TIZIANO VECELLIO,
CALLED TITIAN
(Pieve di Cadore, ca. 1488 –
Venice, 1576)
Ca. 1510
Wood, 65.8 x 83.5 cm
Inv. No. 95

The title of the painting became established at an early date and has traditionally been retained. It refers to the fact that this Madonna is of an unusually dark type. Here the young Titian is still closely modelling his Madonna on those of his teacher Giovanni Bellini. Typical of Bellini's artistic repertoire are the distinctive motif of the fabric hung in the background, the view of a Venetian landscape and the balanced triangular composition. The colours of the main motif return gently and a shade lighter in the landscape, an artistic choice that gives both areas – the intimate closeness of the devotional motif and the idyllic landscape – a prevailing mood of unity. This had also been one of the formal principles of Titian's teacher. The younger artist emancipated himself in another respect: his special ability to model and characterise the volume of the bodies and the surface of the objects using minimal nuances of colour, sparse white highlights and subdued shadow distinguished him from his Venetian contemporaries, among them Giorgione (cf. Cat. Nos. 10, 13), who also studied in Bellini's workshop.

15 ADORATION OF THE TRINITY (LANDAUER ALTAR)

ALBRECHT DÜRER
(Nuremberg, 1471 –
Nuremberg, 1528)
1511
Wood, 135 x 123 cm
Inv. No. 838

In 1501 Matthias Landauer, who had a flourishing business selling the products of his smelter, founded the Zwölfbrüderhaus ("Twelve Brothers House") in Nuremberg. This was an institution that provided a home for twelve needy artisans in their old age. In 1508 the founder commissioned an altarpiece for the newly erected chapel. Dürer had returned a year earlier to Nuremberg from his second trip to Venice, which had been a revelation to him. He chose the more modern form of the altarpiece rather than the late Gothic winged altar. The chapel was dedicated to all the saints, and this resulted in his choice of subject: the Trinity – the Dove of the Holy Spirit, God the Father and Christ – is the focus of attention. Supported by a band of angels presenting instruments of the Passion to Christ, the group hovers above the crowd arranged in a semi-circle around them. Mary leads the group of female saints, among them Barbara (chalice), Catherine (wheel) and Agnes (lamb): behind John the Baptist on the right is a host of prophets and kings of the Old Testament, including David (harp) and Moses (tablets of the Law). The presence at the bottom of a group of members of the sacred and secular Christian community – from popes to a simple monk, from an emperor to representatives of the peasantry (threshing flail) – cannot be explained with All Saints iconography. Their lives have already been weighed in the Last Judgment depicted on the frame, and thus they are members of the "kingdom of God". This concept is based on the writings of St. Augustine (354 – 430 AD). Landauer himself, invited to join by a cardinal, is found in the group at the left edge of the painting. As he did in other cases as well, Dürer expanded his signature by adding a full-length self-portrait in the landscape at the bottom.

The work was acquired in Nuremberg in 1585, but without the original frame designed by Dürer (Nuremberg, Germanisches Nationalmuseum), by Emperor Rudolf II and remains the highlight among the Dürers in the Vienna collection. The Vienna frame is a 19th-century copy of the original.

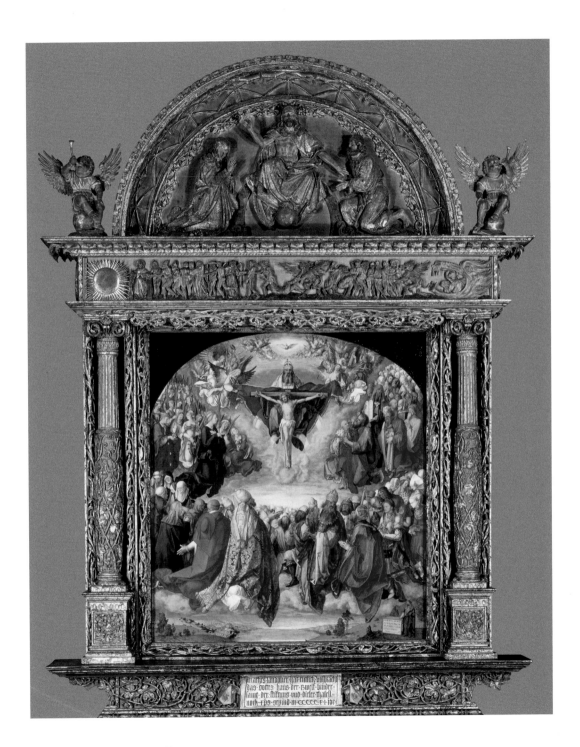

16 ALTARPIECE OF SAINTS THOMAS AND MATTHIAS

BERNAERD (BARENT)
VAN ORLEY
(Brussels, ca. 1492 –
Brussels, 1542)
Ca. 1512
Wood, 140 x 180 cm
Inv. No. 992

In 1512 van Orley received a commission to create a winged altar for a chapel in the church of Notre Dame de Sablon in Brussels. The central panel was acquired for the Vienna gallery in 1809 by Emperor Francis I; the two wings have also been preserved and are now in the Musées royaux des Beaux-Arts de Belgique in Brussels. Orley was commissioned by the local Guild of Masons and Carpenters, who chose the patron saints of their guild, Matthias and Thomas, as the subject. The painter uses a unified space to bring together the two very different lives, but divides the panel into two halves: the clear dividing line is placed in the central foreground, a pillar inspired by a late-Gothic church portal.

After the Ascension of Christ, the Apostles cast lots to choose a successor to Judas, and Matthias was selected to replace him. This event is depicted in the scene at the right in a setting of magnificent fantasy architecture inspired by Renaissance forms. Matthias became the patron saint of carpenters because he was allegedly martyred by having his head chopped off with an axe.

According to legend, Christ appeared to Thomas and told him to build a Roman-style palace for the Indian king Gondophernes (or Guduphara). He continued his missionary efforts but was killed by an Indian high priest who was beside himself. His martyrdom can be seen in the central scene on the left.

In 1518, several years after the completion of this early work, van Orley became court painter to the regent Margaret of Austria. After Jan Gossaert (Cat. No. 26), he shares the distinction with Jan van Scorel as the most important exponent of the first generation of Netherlandish Romanist painters who made study trips to Italy, introducing the new forms they found into northern art.

17 THE ARCHANGEL RAPHAEL WITH TOBIAS, ST. LEONARD AND THE DONOR, LEONARDO DI LORENZO MORELLI

ANDREA D'AGNOLO,
CALLED DEL SARTO
(Florence, 1486 –
Florence, 1530)
1512
Wood, 178 x 153 cm
Inv. No. 182

Raphael accompanied the young Tobias on a journey that he had undertaken to help his father, who had gone blind (Old Testament, Book of Tobit). One day they were resting on the bank of a river when suddenly a huge fish leapt out of the water. Raphael's advice was to catch the fish and preserve its viscera. The liver and heart of the fish were used during the journey, even before Raphael and Tobias, who had meanwhile married, returned to his father. Here the angel finally revealed the purpose of the last of the fish's viscera that remained, its gall. With it Tobias healed his father's blind eyes.

Veneration of Raphael as a guardian angel became established in early Christian times, and the popular theme was in its heyday in the prosperous Florence of the 15th century. Rich merchants donated altarpieces for their sons at an age when the latter were not yet grown but were already undertaking their first commercial travels. In March 1512, the Florentine silk merchant Leonardo di Lorenzo Morelli commissioned this picture for the family chapel of Sta. Lucia in Settimello near Florence.

Almost the entire surface of the panel, which is semicircular at the top, is occupied by Tobias, St. Raphael and St. Leonard, the patron saint of the donor. Morelli himself is kneeling next to the group at the edge of the painting. As he desired, the gentle blue evening sky is opening behind the head of Raphael; Christ bearing his Cross is dynamically portrayed above the group – a dramatic detail that suggests a fundamental stylistic change, as does the expressive coloration: along with his pupils Pontormo and Rosso Fiorentino, Sarto was one of the first Florentine artists to abandon the principles of the High Renaissance – a calm and balanced composition and a striving for ideal beauty and harmony of coloration (cf. *Lamentation of Christ;* KHM, GG, Inv. No. 201).

18 VIRGIN AND CHILD WITH A PEAR

ALBRECHT DÜRER
(Nuremberg, 1471 –
Nuremberg, 1528)
1512
Wood, 49 x 37 cm
Inv. No. 848

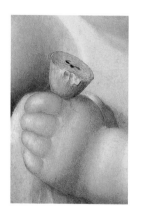

Unusual in the long series of Dürer's depictions of the Madonna, this painting differs in its motivic structure and the painterly rendition of the head of Mary and the infant Jesus. The gently smiling face of the Madonna derives from the Netherlandish tradition, but the posture of the child, his body twisted on its axis, can be found in the early Italian Renaissance. Also of Italian origin is the powerful corporeality of the infant Jesus, which Dürer generously characterises with soft shadows. In his left hand the infant holds the upper end of a pear, which was considered a symbol of virginity.

During his second stay in Venice (1505–1507) Dürer had to a certain degree internalised the ideals of Venetian painting. There is a greater emphasis on painterly rather than graphic representation, and individual details are omitted in favour of the overall impression. The *Virgin and Child with a Pear* was created during a phase of upheaval in Dürer's work: between 1513 and 1516, Dürer turned away from painting for a considerable period, creating important graphic works instead. Shortly before this period began, however, he completed another commissioned painting: he created two idealised portraits, *Charlemagne* and *Emperor Sigismund,* to decorate a room in Nuremberg's "Schoppenhaus", where the imperial regalia were stored before being displayed at the Feast of the Holy Lance, which was celebrated just after Easter. Early 17th-century copies of these decorative paintings are found today in the Treasury of the Kunsthistorisches Museum (GG, Inv. Nos. 2770 and 2771).

19 YOUNG WOMAN IN A BLUE DRESS, WITH FAN

JACOPO NEGRETTI,
CALLED PALMA IL VECCHIO
(Serinalta near Bergamo,
ca. 1480 – Venice, 1528)
Ca. 1512/14
Wood, 63.5 x 51 cm
Inv. No. 63

This frank and open, idealised portrait of a Venetian beauty is uniformly illuminated. Silky surfaces intensify her sensual charisma, with even her hair subordinated to the overall impression of the portrait. The dominance of the blue dress is balanced by the strong skin tone and the elaborately coiffured blonde hair. The young woman's gaze is directed at the observer, who is perhaps enchanted by her appearance, but the deprecatory gesture of her hand keeps him at bay.

Around 1500, the depiction of beautiful women with idealised features and a gentle note of eroticism began developing into a special Venetian type, possibly stimulated by a (now lost) work by Giovanni Bellini. Giorgione (Cat. No. 13) and the young Titian took up the theme, and their works had wide-reaching influence, found with special intensity in the paintings of Palma Vecchio. Both the artists and their patrons were primarily interested in the connection with contemporary lyric poetry, having been influenced by the recent popularity of the *Canzoniere* by Petrarch (1304–1374), in which he celebrated in verse an unrealisable desire for a beautiful woman as well as pure and lasting love.

JOACHIM PATINIER
(Bouvignes or Dinant,
ca. 1475/80 –
Antwerp, 1524)
Ca. 1515
Wood, 59.7 x 76.3 cm
Inv. No. 981

Patinier was the first Netherlandish painter to specialise in the depiction of landscapes, although he always added figures to them. Albrecht Dürer had made his acquaintance during a trip to the Netherlands and mentioned him in 1521 in his diary as "a good landscape painter", thus providing the first documented use of this term in German north of the Alps.

Patinier's landscapes are serious and strict in their composition, never realistic. They are characterised by bizarre, sometimes even geologically impossible cliff formations and cool coloration. *The Baptism of Christ* is one of the major works by the Antwerp painter, who sometimes seems to have been influenced by Hieronymus Bosch and also adapted compositions by Gerard David to his purposes. Here he observes the tradition of an axial structure, with God the Father in the clouds, the Dove of the Holy Spirit and the Baptism of Christ. In the middle distance we see a sermon by John the Baptist. Christ is listening from a distance, still wearing the blue garment that he has laid aside in the foreground. The religious scene and the depiction of a magnificent landscape seem to balance one another – an innovation that influenced the entire development of Flemish landscape painting. Its immediate influence was on Patinier's first successor, Herri met de Bles, who also worked in Antwerp.

GIOVANNI BELLINI
(Venice, ca. 1433 –
Venice, 1516)
1515
Wood, 62 x 79 cm
Inv. No. 97

Giovanni Bellini, who came from an important family of painters, was the son of Jacopo Bellini and the younger brother of Gentile as well as the brother-in-law of Andrea Mantegna (Cat. No. 3). In 1483 he became official painter of the Republic of Venice, and together with his pupils Giorgione and Titian he was one of the founders of the Venetian High Renaissance. He viewed himself almost exclusively as a painter of religious subjects. There are only a few paintings by Bellini in which he deals with mythological themes, and his refusal to paint such a work for the Mantuan patron of the arts Isabella d'Este is legendary. Thus the Vienna portrait of a young woman, which he painted in 1515, a year before his death, is such an exception.

The nude figure is integrated into a system of horizontal and vertical features. She is sitting on a bench that has been covered with a precious carpet, and behind her is a dark-green surface on which a mirror has been hung. On the left a view of a Venetian landscape gives the painting depth. By using the same colours in the principal motif and landscape, Bellini connects the two spheres, and the basic mood of the painting is gentle and unified. In her right hand the young woman is holding another mirror, which is a symbol of vanitas on the one hand and an attribute of Venus Pudica on the other. Using the device of two mirrors, Bellini enables the observer to see two views of the woman's head from a single vantage point, a perspective possible only in painting. In addition, he thus enhances the independence of the woman's action from the view of the beholder – although the physical distance is very small.

In his signature ("Johannes bellinus faciebat M.D.X.V") on the small slip of paper on the right, Bellini is using a formulation by Apelles, considered the greatest painter of antiquity, and handed down by Pliny. This is further evidence of the basic theme of the work: the beauty and creative power of painting.

BACCIO DELLA PORTA,
CALLED
FRA BARTOLOMMEO
(Florence, 1472 –
Florence, 1517)
1516
Wood, 155 x 159 cm
Inv. No. 207

In the late 1490s, impressed by the sermons of the Dominican friar Girolamo Savonarola (1452–1498), Baccio della Porta, who preached against the dissolute life of nobility and clergy, refused to paint secular themes. Having entered the Dominican monastery of San Marco in Florence in 1500, he worked there under the name Fra Bartolommeo. In 1505 he became head of the order's flourishing workshop of painters. On a visit to Rome in 1513, he saw the innovative achievements of Michelangelo and Raphael. His monumental altarpieces combined these ideas with local traditions, bringing the High Renaissance in Florence to its logical conclusion.

Like his other work, this one, which Fra Bartolommeo painted for the church of his own monastery, combines symmetrical structure, monumental figures, graphic clarity alongside fluent painterly aspects, solemn gravity and quiet gestures. The temple interior is depicted in the central perspective typical of the Florentine manner, which creates a formal setting for the scene, viewed slightly from below. In his arms the elderly Simeon is holding the Christ Child, who has been brought to the temple by his parents. He recognises in Him the Messiah and turns towards Mary: "[…] Behold, this [child] is set for the fall and rising again of many in Israel; and for a sign which shall be spoken against; (Yea, a sword shall pierce through thy own soul also,) that the thought of many hearts may be revealed." (Luke 2:34–35.)

23 EMPEROR MAXIMILIAN I WITH HIS FAMILY

BERNHARD STRIGEL
(Memmingen, ca. 1460 –
Memmingen, 1528)
Ca. 1516/20
Wood, 72.8 x 60.4 cm
Inv. No. 832

Bernhard Strigel, the last known member of a successful family of artists from the Allgäu region of southern Germany, held a succession of honorary civic offices in Memmingen beginning in 1512. A much sought-after portraitist, he was soon appointed imperial court painter and finally raised to the peerage.

His painting portrays Emperor Maximilian I and his first wife, Mary of Burgundy (1457–1482), next to their son Philip the Fair, who had died in 1506. Below them are Philip's sons Charles (in the middle) and Ferdinand (on the left). To the right of them is Louis of Hungary, whom Maximilian had adopted in 1515. The inscriptions give a second meaning to the portraits: they identify the subjects as members of the family of Mary Cleophas, who had been venerated as one of the sisters of the Virgin Mary since the early 15th century. Originally the other members of the Virgin's family were on the back of the panel (removed in 1919; KHM, GG, Inv. No. 6411) and on another part (now in private ownership) of the work, which was originally conceived as a diptych.

How the work was commissioned is not completely clear. It is known for certain that Johannes Cuspinian, a Humanist advisor to Maximilian, commissioned the second panel and the back of the first. But perhaps – and this appears more plausible – he commissioned the entire diptych, including the present painting, in 1520, five years after the double wedding that he had helped to negotiate. The selection of figures is certainly a reference to that event. As a proxy for one of his grandsons Maximilian married the sister of Louis, Anna of Hungary, in Vienna in 1515. A reciprocal gesture for the decision taken in 1507 that Louis would marry Archduchess Maria, the sister of Charles and Ferdinand, this successful move on the dynastic chessboard was solemnly celebrated with a double wedding in Vienna and guaranteed the emperor's successors the crowns of Bohemia and Hungary until 1918.

CLEOPHAS FRATER · CARNALIS · IO=
SEPHI · MARITI · DIVAE · VIRG · MARIAE

IACOBVS · MINOR · FFCS · MARA · CLEOPHAE · SOROR·
HIEROSOLIMITANVS · VIRG · MAR · PVTATIVA · MA·
TERTERA · D · NI

IOSEPH · IVSTVS · SIMON · ZELOTES · CONSO=
BRINVS · DNI · NRI ·

71

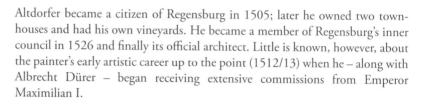

ALBRECHT ALTDORFER
(Regensburg, ca. 1482/85 –
Regensburg, 1538)
1518
Wood, 70 x 37 cm
Inv. No. 6796

Altdorfer became a citizen of Regensburg in 1505; later he owned two town-houses and had his own vineyards. He became a member of Regensburg's inner council in 1526 and finally its official architect. Little is known, however, about the painter's early artistic career up to the point (1512/13) when he – along with Albrecht Dürer – began receiving extensive commissions from Emperor Maximilian I.

Along with three other panels (including the *Entombment of Christ;* KHM, GG, Inv. No. 6427), the *Resurrection of Christ* was originally part of a predella (base of an altarpiece). The twelve larger panels of the wings are still in their place of origin, the Abbey of St. Florian near Linz. In 1508 its provost had commissioned Altdorfer to paint an altar to St. Sebastian. All the other parts of the polyptych – wooden sculptures and shrine – have been lost.

The illumination and use of colour are highly dramatic. Christ appears in a dark scene – actually set at night. His halo is at the same time the rising sun, glowing red in the background. The uniformly formal treatment of the human figures and their setting along with the expressive depiction of the vegetation are striking qualities of the so-called Danube school of painting, which resulted from the early work of Lucas Cranach (Cat. No. 9). Altdorfer became its most important exponent.

25   PORTRAIT OF MAXIMILIAN I

ALBRECHT DÜRER
(Nuremberg, 1471 –
Nuremberg, 1528)
1519
Wood, 74 x 61.5 cm
Inv. No. 825

In 1512 Dürer was asked by Maximilian to participate in extensive artistic projects, which, as the emperor openly admitted, were designed to preserve his posthumous reputation. The project that was most obviously connected with that purpose was the planning of his tomb – never completed – in Innsbruck, and here Dürer was also involved from time to time. In 1518, in a completely different context, he had the opportunity of making a charcoal drawing of the aging Habsburg emperor during the imperial diet at Augsburg. The study (Vienna, Albertina) was the model for a painted portrait, which may have been commissioned by Jakob Fugger, who founded Augsburg's Fuggerei (the world's oldest social settlement) and the Fugger trading company.

Dürer portrays the emperor as an elegant private gentleman. Here the painter adopted an existing type in the tradition of Habsburg portraits (cf. Cat. No. 23) but combined it with incomparable mastery of the demands of the state portrait. The emperor is not wearing the outward signs of his high rank; even the otherwise obligatory neck chain of the Order of the Golden Fleece is not worn on the emperor's body but appears at the upper left in the background. Instead, the desired impression of power and dignity is provided by the way the emperor fills the frame, the precious fabrics and the brilliantly painted fur collar, Timelessness and distance are suggested by the monochrome background. The monumentality of Maximilian's physical appearance has imperial character; the precise depiction of quiet melancholy and fatigue on his face in no way diminishes the extraordinary importance of the subject. Several interpretations have been proposed for the pomegranate in his hand, all of which may be correct: it may be a private replacement for the imperial orb, a reference to the myth of Persephone and thus to the fact that Maximilian had already died, and/or an allusion to the conquest of Granada by Christian armies in 1492.

26 ST. LUKE PAINTING THE MADONNA

JAN GOSSAERT,
CALLED MABUSE
(Maubeuge [?], ca. 1478 –
Antwerp [Middelburg?], 1532)
Ca. 1520
Wood, 109.5 x 82 cm
Inv. No. 894

According to a legend documented in a written source only since the 6th century, Christian painting began with St. Luke, the author of the third of the four Gospels. He is said to have painted the first portrait of Mary, who posed for him, perhaps in the house of John. This is how countless painters' guilds on both sides of the Alps got their name.

Here Gossaert makes a striking change to the iconography that was customary up to this time: while the painter is still shown during a realistic, domestic portrait sitting, Mary is depicted as Queen of Heaven accompanied by angels in a religious setting of architecture inspired by contemporary Italian models. An angel as a symbol of divine inspiration guides St. Luke's hand.

Gossaert derived the name "Mabuse" from his hometown of Maubeuge, a small French city, today on the Belgian border. In 1503 he was mentioned for the first time as a master in the Guild of St. Luke at Antwerp. Four years later he vanished for a time without a trace. On 14 January 1509, he arrived in Rome, accompanying a diplomatic delegation led by his employer, Philip of Burgundy (the admiral of Zeeland and the illegitimate son of Duke Philip the Good). He remained in the Eternal City for several months, a period that he took advantage of by eagerly studying the sculpture and architecture of classical antiquity, as evidenced by a drawing of the Colosseum (Berlin, Museum of Prints and Drawings), among others. Probably he had the privilege of viewing works that Michelangelo and Raphael had created for the Vatican. After his return to the Netherlands, Gossaert successfully combined new and clearly foreign elements of Italianate style with local traditions, putting himself in the forefront of Dutch Romanism.

FRANCESCO MAZZOLA,
CALLED PARMIGIANINO
(Parma, 1503 –
Casalmaggiore, 1540)
Ca. 1523/24
Wood, Dm 24.4 cm
Inv. No. 286

This artist, who came from Parma, is considered one of the most progressive painters in the 1st half of the 16th century in Upper Italy, Parmigianino's work provides a transition from the Renaissance to Mannerism, and the effects of his delicate and extravagant formal language were still being felt in the art of Rudolf II's court in Prague (ca. 1600).

Parmigianino presented this self-portrait, painted on a convex wooden surface, along with two other small-format works to Pope Clement VII in the summer of 1524. He was ultimately unsuccessful in this attempt to gain prestigious and lucrative commissions from the Vatican, but even in the 16th century this unusual portrait was a widely recognised testimony to his talent. The work had a number of other prominent owners before entering the collection of Rudolf II in 1608, among them Pietro Aretino, Andrea Palladio and Alessandro Vittoria.

"More like an angel than a man" is Giorgio Vasari's description of Parmigianino in his artists' lives of 1568, and thus the 21-year-old presents himself to the viewer. His artist's hand (actually his left hand, although it seems to be his right) is distorted but impressively enlarged in the foreground, but he excludes the depiction of his head from the optical effect of the convex mirror. The bare studio in the background, however, is reflected by the barber's mirror, by this time already old-fashioned, with which the artist was working here. Another ingenious aspect is seen at the extreme right edge of the painting: a gilt frame, itself a part of the artwork that is currently being created on Parmigianino's easel.

28 JOHANNES KLEBERGER

ALBRECHT DÜRER
(Nuremberg, 1471 –
Nuremberg, 1528)
1526
Wood, 37 x 36.6 cm
Inv. No. 850

Johannes Kleberger was an international merchant who is believed to have returned to his hometown of Nuremberg in 1525, a year before this extravagant portrait, unique among Dürer's works, was painted. A successful businessman with excellent connections to the French court, he had been living abroad since 1521, first in Bern and soon afterwards in Lyon, and had become one of the most important financiers of King Francis I. There is perhaps a relationship between Dürer's commission for this painting and the marriage of Kleberger to Felizitas Imhoff in 1528: Felizitas, the daughter of the well-known Humanist and friend of Dürer, Willibald Pirckheimer, had been widowed in 1526. Pirckheimer had initially sought to prevent the remarriage of his daughter. Kleberger, who was repeatedly described as a brilliant opportunist, may have used this valuable artwork, which in its conception would have suited the Humanist, as a tool in his courtship. To Pirckheimer's dismay, the bridegroom was to leave his new wife a year later.

Kleberger is looking to his right in a decisive and concentrated manner. The almost unpleasantly moving paradox of the composition quickly becomes apparent: the bust, which appears to be pulsing with life, is cut off sharply at the bottom and is balanced in the circular opening of a wall. Only the dark background lessens the impression of instability. The Latin inscription is similar to that on classical portrait medallions, giving the name, origin and age of the subject as well as the cabbalistic sign of the *sol in corde leonis,* an expression of his astrological constellation at birth, which promised unusual power and strength. In consultation with Kleberger, Dürer used the four spandrel areas for other references to the character and position of his patron. At the left above, the astrological sign for Leo surrounded by six stars; to its right is the artist's signature. At the left below a figurative coat of arms: three green clover-leaves above a yellow triple hill; to its right the clover-leaves are repeated, but with the addition of a helmet to "ennoble" them.

29 MADONNA AND CHILD WITH SAINTS CATHERINE AND THOMAS (SACRA CONVERSAZIONE)

LORENZO LOTTO
(Venice, ca. 1480 –
Loreto, 1556/57)
1528/30
Canvas, 113.5 x 152 cm
Inv. No. 101

In the Venetian painting of the early 16th century, a new type of *sacra conversazione* became established alongside the older type (Cat. No. 5), in which the figures were depicted in an architectural setting. The new type was often in landscape format and set outdoors under an open sky. There are several examples of this in Lotto's work, which was inspired in particular by Palma Vecchio, with whom Lotto was on friendly terms, according to the artists' biographer Vasari. Palma Vecchio had abandoned the conventional hierarchic arrangement of figures and developed more intimate compositions seen from a closer distance. Lotto, who was considered the most individualist of the Venetian artists of his generation, continued these tendencies. In their gestures, glances and posture, his figures were much closer together than those of the painters before him.

The backdrop of the picture is a gently illuminated landscape in the distance. Mary and the Child, Catherine, Thomas and an angel are seated in the shadow of a tree. Lotto decisively changes the time-honoured type: the picture is marked not by the tranquillity of the High Renaissance but by the sensitive expressiveness of early Mannerism. A continuous and nervous stream of movement sweeps across the picture, from the arms of the angel crowning the Madonna to the hand of the Child reaching for the book to the head of Catherine as she looks towards the devout Apostle, who with his intimate eye contact with Mary leads the viewer back to the Virgin. The cool and scarcely Venetian coloration – found throughout Lotto's work – is rooted in the painting of Bergamo, where he spent most of his life, but also in the art of Dürer.

ALESSANDRO BONVICINO,
CALLED
MORETTO DA BRESCIA
(Brescia, ca. 1498 –
Brescia, 1554)
Ca. 1530
Canvas, 200 x 139 cm
Inv. No. 61

Beginning in the 1520s, Moretto da Brescia received numerous commissions in Upper Italy. Until the late 1530s his works are remarkable for their elegant synthesis of various painting styles: he combines Giorgione's Venetian style of coloration and surface treatment with Lorenzo Lotto's sharp delineation of light and subjective approach.

There is evidence of the veneration of St. Justina in Upper Italy as early as the 5th century; Benedictine monks later spread the cult of the patron saint of Padua across the whole of Europe. Beginning in the early 15th century, she is usually depicted as a young princess in a long dress and cloak, and carrying a palm branch. Moretto further emphasises her virginity with the presence of a unicorn.

This painting, which in early inventories was attributed at various times to both Titian and Raphael, is considered a major work of the High Renaissance in Upper Italy. Statuesque in her tranquillity, the saint also reflects the work of Raphael and thus Roman art of the time. The connection between the saints, their attributes and the (unknown) donor appears to be quite close so that this devotional image also has somewhat the atmosphere of a love idyll. Taken together, such details as the vertically falling ends of the scarf tied around her waist, which gleam with a silvery light, the standing posture, which imitates the art of antiquity, Justina's palm branch and the animal's horn create a strong compositional structure that sets the saint off against the kneeling donor, despite the harmony of the composition.

31 JUPITER AND IO

ANTONIO ALLEGRI,
CALLED CORREGGIO
(Correggio, 1489/94 –
Correggio, 1534)
Ca. 1530
Canvas, 163.5 x 74 cm
Inv. No. 274

When Io fled from Jupiter – in Greek and Roman mythology the king of gods and man, the master of Heaven and Earth – he summoned dark clouds in broad daylight in order to keep the object of his desire from escaping and to seduce her in all secrecy, because he feared the revenge of his jealous wife, Juno. Using a narrow upright format, Correggio focuses the passionate encounter on the view of the delicate nude back, placing it in a setting that is warm and humid. With great elegance he depicts the erotic union of the god with Io, the mortal daughter of the river god Inachus: Jupiter's face shimmers softly through the grey fog as he kisses Io, while his hand gently grasps her waist; the supposed victim seems to have abandoned any thought of escape. The deer drinking in the bottom right corner gives the erotic motif a trace of Christian decorum: "As the hart panteth after the water brooks, so panteth my soul after thee, O God." (Ps. 42:1.)

Correggio's ability to combine a mystical depiction of nature with the classical figural ideal and the expression of sublime emotion made especially his later works important forerunners of Baroque artistic principles.

The present painting was created along with *The Abduction of Ganymede* (Cat. No. 32), *Leda and the Swan* (Berlin, Picture Gallery) and *Danae* (Rome, Galleria Borghese) on a commission from Duke Federico Gonzaga of Mantua, who most likely gave the two paintings that are now in Vienna to Emperor Charles V as a gift. There was probably a certain reason for doing so: the political significance of depictions of mythological or historical rape scenes. They were widely accepted as metaphors of absolute power, which ideally, however, should have a beneficent effect. This would explain the willing consent of the victim in the present painting.

ANTONIO ALLEGRI,
CALLED CORREGGIO
(Correggio, 1489/94 –
Correggio, 1534)
Ca. 1530
Canvas, 163.5 x 70.5 cm
Inv. No. 276

The legend of Ganymede, the son of the founder of Troy, Tros, has had a homoerotic quality since Homer, because the Ionian poet for the first time clearly identified the lover of "the fairest youth of all that breath'd" (*Iliad*, 20:217) as Zeus. According to Homer, the god transformed himself into an eagle, abducted the object of his desire, and took Ganymede as cupbearer to Mount Olympus. The youth was to be granted immortal life, and in the end, Ganymede found his destiny as a sign of the zodiac (Aquarius).

This tale poses a particular challenge to an artist, regardless of the medium: how to create a convincing portrayal of an eagle lifting an adolescent and soaring effortless into the sky. Correggio chose a narrow upright format, as he had done for the painting's companion piece (Cat. No. 31), giving the composition a vertical character. Looking up in surprise, the sheep-dog forms the prelude to the movement: the viewer's gaze is directed skywards, up over the tree-stump until Ganymede's head, turned towards the viewer, interrupts the movement, while the eagle's tongue delightedly licks the future lover's arm. Correggio visually anchored the group on all sides: the eagle's wings are cropped, the tree on the left "supports" Ganymede from below, and the youth's delicate leg "rests" on a range of gentle hills in the background. Only Ganymede's robe, which has been blown loose by the current, breaks the static equilibrium of the group and thus further enhances the impression of soaring flight.

For the history of the commission, provenance and interpretation cf. Cat. No. 31.

LUCAS CRANACH THE ELDER
(Kronach, 1472 –
Weimar, 1553)
Ca. 1530
Wood, 87 x 56 cm
Inv. No. 858

The Old Testament heroine Judith succeeded through her courage and cunning in entering the tent of general Holofernes at his camp outside the city of Bethulia and in seducing and then beheading him, thus ending the military threat against her people. At the time Cranach painted this portrait of the heroine, he had been working as court painter to the elector of Saxony for almost twenty years. The tax records of the city of Wittenberg list him as its wealthiest citizen. All the known versions of the half-length portraits of Judith from Cranach's large workshop were painted around the year 1530. This striking concentration was apparently related to the founding of the Schmalkaldic League: Judith became a symbol of armed Protestant resistance to Charles V and his Catholic armies.

Given this connection with contemporary history, Judith's character as a man-killing *femme cruelle,* emphasised in other paintings, becomes secondary. Nevertheless, Cranach's Judith also shows a trace of eroticism. Her long, flowing hair, costly and fashionable clothing, low décolleté with gold jewellery and the delicate gestures of her hands create tension with the openly displayed head of the enemy general and the erect sword she demonstratively holds in her right hand. But this is only one side of the story, because on the other hand Cranach's choice of colours results in a subtle unity: the deadly character of this Old Testament murder is depicted in a variety of carefully nuanced shades of red. The style of Cranach's Wittenberg paintings – regardless of the subject – is unmistakable: his compositions are always two-dimensional without reference to the surrounding space and usually also have a decorative effect.

91

34 BOW-CARVING AMOR

FRANCESCO MAZZOLA,
CALLED PARMIGIANINO
(Parma, 1503 –
Casalmaggiore, 1540)
Ca.1534/35
Wood, 135 x 65.3 cm
Inv. No. 275

Since 1578 Emperor Rudolf II had been trying with dogged persistence to acquire this painting, which meanwhile was in the collection of the Spanish king. It was only in 1605, with the help of his agent Hans Khevenhüller, that he finally succeeded in acquiring the coveted work.

Probably created in Parma in 1534/35, the painting is among the key works of Upper Italian Mannerism, and Parmigianino had played an important role in the development of the style. The great popularity of his concept for this painting is attested to by some fifty known copies (cf. the one by Joseph Heintz; KHM, GG, Inv. No. 1588).

Completely in keeping with the contemporary concept, which was sometimes accompanied by homoerotic desires, Amor appears here not as a small child but as an adolescent youth. With the back turned towards the viewer, the almost uniformly illuminated body of the messenger of love fills the entire height of the composition. His penetrating glance (reminiscent of Amor's arrows) looks seductively from the painting. The weapon he is making in order to spread joy and pain in equal measure rests carelessly on the two books, in a gesture in triumph over their learned contents. Two putti, seen between Amor's straddled legs, are wrestling behind him. According to one interpretation, the victor in their proxy struggle between palpable desire and quiet longing has not yet been decided.

Parmigianino brilliantly characterises the different surfaces: Amor's hair, which is artistically coiffed in delicate curls, the soft wings elegantly attached to his body and, finally, the skin of the three protagonists, the colour of which powerfully dominates the picture. This late work by the artist, who died in 1540 at the age of only 39, is distinguished by the smooth, brightly illuminated bodies and finely worked details.

35   GIRL IN A FUR

TIZIANO VECELLIO,
CALLED TITIAN
(Pieve di Cadore, ca. 1488 –
Venice, 1576)
Ca. 1535
Canvas, 95 x 63 cm
Inv. No. 89

This young woman repeatedly posed for Titian. All the paintings in which she appears, including the famous *Venus of Urbino* (1538, Florence, Uffizi Galleries), were created for Francesco Maria della Rovere, the nephew of Pope Julius II and Duke of Urbino from 1508, or for his son Guidobaldi. The present work is probably from that same period.

The charming, erotically charged appearance of the unknown woman is not to be understood as a portrait: here Titian is celebrating a general concept of beauty, which was enhanced by contemporary lyric poetry under the influence of Petrarch. Along with the revealing posture of the beautiful woman, the main motif is the stimulating combination of fur and skin, an artistic strategy used before Titian by Giorgione in his *Laura* (Cat. No. 13). The precious fur cloak has slid down the girl's right shoulder, exposing her breast. She is still holding the cloak to her body with her right hand, but she has made a first beginning. The ambivalence of her posture is based on a classical model: the type of the Venus Pudica resonates in Titian's painting. The precious jewellery – strings of pearls, ear-rings, bracelet and ring – creates distance and also opens another level of meaning in the picture as a portrait of a Venetian courtesan.

In 1630 the painting found a famous admirer: Rubens copied Titian's work, which was then in English ownership, and later further developed the older artist's innovation in his own style. From Titian's comparatively reserved Renaissance portrait, Rubens developed an equally complex Baroque alternative in a full-length portrait of his second wife, Helena Fourment (Cat. No. 73).

HANS HOLBEIN
THE YOUNGER
(Augsburg, 1497 –
London, 1543)
1536
Wood, 65.4 x 40.7 cm
Inv. No. 881

On 29 January 1536, Anne Boleyn, the second wife of England's King Henry VIII, had a miscarriage at Hampton Court Palace. Four months later she was sentenced to death on the charge of alleged unfaithfulness and executed the day before the king's engagement to Jane Seymour. The later queen had come to Henry's court in 1530 and served her two predecessors as lady-in-waiting. Jane Seymour is the only one of the wives of Henry VIII buried together with the king at Windsor Castle – not least because she was the mother of the long-awaited and only heir to the throne. She died in October 1537 while giving birth to him.

Hans Holbein had made a career for himself in Basel. He had lived in London since 1532 and was appointed court painter to the English monarch in 1536, the year of the royal wedding. The monochrome background of the painting is a concession to the demands of the court portrait. In contrast to the technique he used for other subjects, Holbein conceived such portraits with a pronounced flatness, thus giving them a formal character. Jane Seymour's precious jewellery, her garment and her pale features are bathed in an even light and presented in every detail – an old-fashioned method that had been superseded by a full-toned chiaroscuro not only in Italian painting (with which Holbein must have been well-acquainted). However, it is precisely this plain objectivity that creates the necessary distance from the viewer.

MAERTEN VAN HEEMSKERCK
(Heemskerck, 1498 –
Haarlem, 1574)
After 1540
Wood, 56.3 x 106.5 cm
Inv. No. 990

On his many journeys, Bacchus (Greek: Dionysus), the Greek and Roman god of wine and fertility, was accompanied by Maenads and Satyrs, his attribute the panther, and goats. Together, they indulged themselves in an ecstasy stimulated by wine and dance. In the art of classical antiquity, the wine-god's outward appearance as a nude, soft and often drunken ruler became early established.

The present painting in landscape format shows Bacchus as the main figure in a triumphal procession. He is to proceed through the arch visible at the left edge of the painting on his way to his final destination, the round temple situated on a hill in the background. Bacchus is seated in the chariot, enthroned atop a wine barrel. His entourage is equally intoxicated; even the animal pulling the chariot is no longer up to its task. Beneath the animal, a Satyr has fallen to the ground and vomited; a mirror held by a gleeful child reveals the mishap to the viewer. Further to the front of the procession dancers and acrobatics are the centre of attention. The dark-skinned figures are a reference to the mythical journey of Bacchus to India but also serve to punctuate the lighter brown shades used by the artist with varying intensity. Details depicted in their full materiality, such as the Maenads' thyrsus (a staff wrapped in leafy vine and ivy), the drinking vessel in the wine-god's left hand, wine jars, musical instruments and pieces of jewellery as well as the architectural elements provide the necessary compositional counterbalance to the soft fleshy depictions of the figures.

Maerten van Heemskerck was part of a second generation of Netherlandish painters who made extensive study visits to Rome. The impressions he gained there are clearly visible in the present painting: the foot of a colossal statue in the foreground on the left, the Satyr figures at the arch and the round temple in the background are based on classical models.

TIZIANO VECELLIO,
CALLED TITIAN
(Pieve di Cadore, ca. 1488 –
Venice, 1576)
1543
Canvas, 242 x 361 cm
Inv. No. 73

Compared with the overall development of Upper Italian painting (Cat. Nos. 27, 29, 34), Titian's short Mannerist phase was weaker in its expressiveness, and in early art criticism it received a cool reception, unjustly so from the viewpoint of today. This *Ecce Homo,* created for the Flemish merchant Giovanni d'Anna, is Titian's major work of the period. For a long time it was seen primarily as a legendary compendium of contemporary prominent figures: it was thought that Pilate had the features of Pietro Aretino; the magnificently dressed older man in the right foreground was the Venetian doge in office at the time, Pietro Lando; the Ottoman knight behind him was Sultan Süleyman II; and farther to the right is his military opponent, Alfonso d'Avalos (Venice had defeated the Turks at Tunis in 1535). The young woman dressed in white was thought to be Titian's daughter. In contrast to the art of the southern Netherlands, this scene in which the crowd demands that Christ be put to death (Luke 23:13–25; John 19:13–16) was rarely depicted in Italian painting. The Flemish origin of the client probably explains the unusual choice of subject.

Titian's brilliant stage management focuses all attention on the figure of Christ, even though it has been strikingly placed at the edge of the painting. A young man in complete dismay in the left foreground sets the compositional mood. The soldier seen from the rear leads the viewer's gaze up the steps to the protagonist. The double-eagle of the Holy Roman Empire on his shield and the signature on the parchment to the right of it with the addition "eques ces[aris]" are a gesture of homage to the imperial court, of which Titian had become the official painter in 1533. Pilate's indecisive posture points to his ambiguous historical role; his head is turned towards the rude crowd, pressing forward and again directing the viewer's gaze towards Christ. The soldier clad in dark-red velvet at the centre of the painting has a transitional function, dosing off the dramatic scene to his left and leading towards the group of curious spectators on his right.

39 HOLY FAMILY WITH ST. ANNE AND THE INFANT ST. JOHN

AGNOLO DI COSIMO,
CALLED BRONZINO
(Monticelli near Florence,
1503 – Florence, 1572)
Ca. 1545/46
Wood, 124.5 x 99.5 cm
Inv. No. 183

Completely in contrast to the principles of Venetian painting, which made colour the dominant means of expression, Renaissance painting in Florence always gave priority to the drawing as the means of expressing artistic invention. Thus there was a demand that the contours in painting be clear and sometimes even sharp. Bronzino's works are considered the epitome of Florentine *disegno* and, at the same time, its final pinnacle, which had already assumed the character of Mannerism. Bronzino, who was a pupil of Jacopo Pontormo and thus extremely familiar with the works of Michelangelo, served for many years as court painter to the Medici. He created decorations (now lost) for numerous theatrical works and festive occasions and supplied brilliant designs for the Medici tapestry factory.

In his composition Bronzino organises the group in close proximity to one another in the foreground. Nevertheless the figures are arranged next to and behind each other in a way that makes them easy to recognise. The infant St. John is in the foremost position, his gaze and gesture pointing to the infant Jesus, who is depicted frontally. Behind them stands St. Mary, who is holding her son's arm in a loving gesture. The composition is extended by St. Anne and St. Joseph, who stand out from the central group of three because of their more natural skin colour. More than in almost any other of his works, Bronzino has emphasised the sharply outlined and sculptural figures almost to the point of stony coldness, especially in the case of the two boys. This artistic decision is also an example of *paragone* (Italian: comparison) – the competition, discussed in art theory at the time, between painting and sculpture to see which could create the better depiction of three-dimensional forms. Here Bronzino creates exciting contrasts: the coolness and clarity of his composition as opposed to the intimate familiar atmosphere; soft and gentle movements contrasted with formal severity and abstraction; turning away from natural models on the one hand but depicting all of their details on the other.

PIETER AERTSEN
(Amsterdam, 1508 –
Amsterdam, 1575)
1552
Wood, 60 x 101.5 cm
Inv. No. 6927

Starting in the mid-16th century, Aertsen developed a new type of Netherlandish painting with his depictions of kitchens and markers. In most cases he integrated into them Christian scenes, which, however, are always conspicuously smaller and placed in the background of the composition. German art historians invented the term "manieristische Umkehrung" (Mannerist reversal) for this new development.

In this early example, such a scene is at the left edge of the painting, sharply set off by the contour of the dark wall that separates the foreground from the background: "[…] But Martha was cumbered about much serving, and came to him, and said, Lord, dost thou not care that my sister hath left me to serve alone? Bid her therefore that she help me. And Jesus answered and said unto her, Martha, Martha, thou art careful and troubled about many things: But one thing is needful: and Mary hath chosen that good part, which shall not be taken away from her." (Luke 10:40–42.) The central phrase in this passage can be read on the mantlepiece: "Maria heeft wtuercoren dat beeste deel." A tradition dating back to St. Augustine identifies the two sisters with the principles of the *vita activa* (Martha) and the *vita contemplativa* (Mary). Here, however, they are not to be understood as opposites but rather as complementary, creating a whole in the tasks of Christian action and thought.

In the foreground, Aertsen has masterfully depicted an assemblage of the characteristic objects of daily life: bread on a plate, various pitchers and jugs, a leg of venison and a bouquet of flowers as the principal motifs, carefully folded documents and a money pouch hung on the door of a massive chest in the foreground. True to the biblical story, these are objects from the affluent household of Mary. At the same time, however, they are also the requisites for a *vanitas* still life.

GIOVANNI BATTISTA
MORONI
(Albino near Bergamo,
1520/24 – Bergamo, 1578)
1552
Canvas, 87.5 x 70 cm
Inv. No. 78

Moroni met Alessandro Vittoria (1525–1608), who had repeatedly worked with Jacopo Sansovino, Andrea Palladio and Paolo Veronese, during the Council of Trent. A short time earlier, the painter had been hired to decorate the rooms where the Council was to meet. Although Moroni also painted religious pictures, he was one of the very few artists in Italy at the time to specialise in portraits. In his biography of Venetian artists, which was published in 1648, Carlo Ridolfi reports that Titian had suggested to several high Venetian officials travelling to Bergamo that they have their portraits painted by Moroni because his work was "true and natural". Such realistic tendencies were already present in the art of Bergamo, but they are found more strongly in Moroni's case because of the influence of German and Netherlandish painting.

In contrast to the attempts of artists since Renaissance times to conceal the elements of craftsmanship in their profession, Vittoria is apparently facing the viewer in his work clothes. This is further emphasised by his rolled-up sleeve, the uncoiffured look of his hair and the "snapshot" quality of the scene, and yet Moroni undermines all this with the shining, almost silky appearance of the dark fabric of Vittoria's clothing. The sculptor is holding a male torso of antiquity at a respectful distance in his hands, but Moroni's use of colour weakens the formal impression of distance: the thickly applied white of the torso is repeated on the sleeve and on the collar of Vittoria's shirt. This innovative "professional portrait" of an artist colleague influenced Titian with regard to both form and content in his famous portrait of Jacopo Strada (ca. 1567/68; Cat. No. 51).

42 LORENZO SORANZO

JACOPO ROBUSTI,
CALLED TINTORETTO
(Venice, 1518 –
Venice, 1594)
1553
Canvas, 114 x 95.5 cm
Inv. No. 308

The subject of this portrait was named city treasurer in 1551, was director of the Venetian auditor's office starting in 1555, and several years later was head of the public health authority, Soranzo's age can be found beneath his initials on what may be a balustrade in the left foreground.

Here Tintoretto has used a type of composition that served Titian well: the 35-year-old Soranzo is seen in three-quarter view, clad in a coat with fur trim. His upper body turned slightly to the right, he is looking in the opposite direction. Tintoretto uses richly varied lighting to focus our attention on Soranzo's hands, but especially on his face. But without abandoning the essential formal features of portraiture that had been established in conservative Venice, the artist creates something clearly new: freed from outward signs of his social standing, the patrician appears not only as an individual in his outward appearance but also bestowed with specific characteristics that are depicted in a remarkably gentle and subtle manner. Captured as though in a snapshot, the stylised movement contributes to the dynamic, even somewhat unstable mood of the work.

The commission to paint this portrait attests to the rising esteem in which Tintoretto was held, even though he was never to attain the social (and economic) status of his rival Titian.

43   ADORATION OF THE MAGI

JACOPO DA PONTE,
CALLED JACOPO BASSANO
(Bassano, ca. 1510/15 –
Bassano, 1592)
Ca. 1555
Canvas, 92.3 x 117.5 cm
Inv. No. 361

Although Jacopo da Ponte's flourishing workshop, which he opened in 1539, was located in the minor provincial town of Bassano near Venice, he became one of the most influential 16th century painters in the entire Veneto region. First trained by his father, he studied in Venice from 1530 to 1535 before returning to Bassano, his home town. He was a pioneer in both landscape and genre painting. His sons – Francesco, Giambattista, Leandro and Gerolamo, who successively joined his workshop – followed successfully in their father's foot-steps. Bassano's works of the 1550s show the increasing influence of Mannerist achievements from Upper Italy (cf. Cat. Nos. 27, 29, 34) and Venice (cf. Cat. No. 45). The figures in the present *Adoration* also have elongated, unnaturally proportioned limbs; the composition is marked by indistinct spatial relation-ships and an exciting contrast between the reverent intimacy of the scene and its depiction in cool, restless coloration. In addition, Bassano combines two iconographic trends: the northern tradition of depicting the birth and adoration in the stable of Bethlehem in keeping with the biblical text and the modern Venetian version, which transferred the scene into an architectural setting of imitated classical forms.

PAOLO CALIARI,
CALLED VERONESE
(Verona, 1528 –
Venice, 1588)
Ca. 1555
Canvas, 173 x 364 cm
Inv. No. 40

Samuel had been sent to see Jesse and his sons in Bethlehem in order to anoint the successor to Saul, who had fallen from God's favour, as king of Israel. In order to conceal his true intentions, he was to take a young cow with him – the impressive head can be seen on the right – and to invite Jesse and his sons to the sacrifice. Only the youngest son, David, did not initially come because he was keeping the sheep. Samuel ordered Jesse to fetch the shepherd boy, who can be seen in the background hurrying in from the left. "[…] And the LORD said, Arise, anoint him: for this [is] he. Then Samuel took the horn of oil, and anointed him in the midst of his brethren. […]" (1 Sam. 16:12–13).

Veronese painted this early work during his first years in Venice. He came to that city in 1553, working primarily for the upper classes. To realise his Mannerist principles, he used the landscape format in the following narrative strategy: in front of a dark background and without any attempt to create greater depth, Veronese has grouped the actors tightly, overlapping them and creating surprising relationships. The central action becomes clear only after study because the viewer is initially distracted by the drama of the secondary figures, dressed in the finest Venetian fashions. Two figures in the foreground with their backs turned (a device called *repoussoir*) lead our gaze to the kneeling David – on the left the elderly man with a staff and on the right the woman with a baby – but Veronese's skilful use of colour works against our making a rapid reading of his composition.

Architectural features embedded in the landscape sections suggest the power of renewal in the depicted action: on the left the pathway is flanked by ruins; on the right there is a magnificent new structure. The latter, regardless of its intended use, is clearly based on contemporary works by Palladio, whose architectural language Veronese began using in his paintings in the 1550s. By the end of the decade he was himself involved in one of Palladio's projects, decorating the Villa Barbaro (1561 ff.).

45 SUSANNA AND THE ELDERS

JACOPO ROBUSTI,
CALLED TINTORETTO
(Venice, 1518 –
Venice, 1594)
Ca. 1555/56
Canvas, 146.6 x 193.6 cm
Inv. No. 1530

Every day the wife of the wealthy Joakim, Susanna, went into the orchard to take a bath. Before long she inflamed the secret lust of two of her husband's guests: "[…] they perverted their own mind and turned away their eyes that they might not look unto heaven, nor remember just judgments." (Sus. 1:9.) One day the two judges were lying in wait for her, but Susanna rejected their wish to lie with her. Driven by their desire for revenge, they accused Susanna of adultery. She had already been condemned to death when the young Daniel questioned the accusers separately about the particular circumstances of the act and thus exposed them as liars. Susanna was rehabilitated while the two old men were sentenced to death.

Subtly lit and in a setting of richly varied chiaroscuro, Susanna's beauty occupies the foreground of the painting. Absorbed in her mirror image, she is yet unaware of the two intruders – unlike the viewer, who is thus forced into the position of a voyeur. Distorted perspectives, strong light contrasts and the dynamic retreat into the depths of the vast orchard are characteristics of Mannerism, and Tintoretto became its most prominent Venetian exponent. In an impressive manner, the Italian painter relegates the educational potential of the tale to the background, although from the viewpoint of the Catholic Church it would have been of compelling necessity to emphasise it. The animal symbolism, understood only by insiders, hardly reduces the sensuous pleasures: the stag at the left rear stands for lust, the ducks are reminders of fidelity, and the magpie sitting on a branch above Susanna's head is a reference to the imminent slander of the protagonist.

PIETER BRUEGEL THE ELDER
(Breda?, ca. 1526/30 –
Brussels, 1569)
1560
Wood, 118 x 161 cm
Inv. No. 1017

From a bird's-eye view – the only way Bruegel could legibly fit in the impressive number of figures – the viewer looks down onto a wide square with a transition from an urban to a rural setting at the edges. On the right the view opens onto a long street laid out in central perspective and leading to the city centre, where a church steeple (or town-hall tower) soars into the sky. The battlement-crowned building at the edge of the square towards the city opens into an arcade running parallel to the course of the stream. At the left edge of the painting, an idyllic village appears on the horizon. Children – more than 230 in all – are occupied with 83 different games. The whole city seems to be theirs. Bruegel gives the beholder an encyclopaedic view of the children's games of his time. The tininess of the figures and scenes forces a viewer seeking to decipher all the games to study the individual parts of the painting slowly and minutely – an entertaining pastime. However, some modern scholars have refused to accept such a humanistic-oriented, "simple" interpretation: the seemingly useless children's activities have been regarded – probably incorrectly – as a parable for the senselessness and foolishness of human behaviour.

GIUSEPPE ARCIMBOLDO
(Milan, 1527 – Milan, 1593)
1563
Wood, 67 x 50.8 cm
Inv. No. 1589

The Milan-born painter Giuseppe Arcimboldo, who numbered several arch-bishops of that city among his ancestors, was early in the employ of the later Emperor Ferdinand I, working with his father on the decoration of Milan Cathedral. Starting in 1562 he was imperial court painter in Vienna and Prague. In addition to his work as a portraitist, he was praised for his achievements as director and decorator of courtly tournaments and wedding celebrations. However, in 1563 he created a series of paintings of the seasons, and their uniqueness is responsible for the posthumous reputation of the painter, who was rediscovered in the 19th century. Two other paintings of the series have been preserved in addition to the present *Summer*: *Winter* (KHM, GG, Inv. No. 1590) and *Spring (?)* (Madrid, Real Academia de Bellas Artes de San Fernando). A later (1572) complete version of the series is in the Louvre in Paris.

Another series, created in 1566 and depicting the four elements *Fire* (KHM, GG, Inv. No. 1585), *Water* (KHM, GG, Inv. No. 427), *Air* and *Earth* is important in understanding the season paintings. All of these heads were created according to the same unique principle: they are composed of plants, animals and objects appropriate to the respective theme, without a single natural feature of the human face. In 1569 the humanist Giovanni Baptista Fonteo wrote several poems dedicated to Maximilian II, which are key to understanding the project. Based on the Aristotelian philosophy of the comparability of the micro- and macrocosms, the poems formulate all-encompassing praise for the ruler. The emperor has power over the state and people, and thus over nature and the world. There is perfect harmony between the "seasons" and the "elements": summer and fire are hot and dry, winter and water cold and wet, whereas spring and air are hot and wet, autumn and earth cold and dry.

PIETER BRUEGEL THE ELDER
(Breda?, ca. 1526/30 –
Brussels, 1569)
1563
Wood, 114 x 155 cm
Inv. No. 1026

"[…] Go to, let us build us a city and a tower, whose top may reach unto heaven; and let us make us a name […]. And the LORD came down to see the city and the tower […]. And he said: […] let us go down, and there confound their language, that they may not understand one another's speech. […] and they left off to build the city." (Gen. 11:4–8.) King Nimrod, who appears as builder along with his entourage at the bottom left of the painting, is not mentioned in the biblical text. Only the Jewish historian Flavius Josephus, who collaborated with the Romans, combined records from different sources to create the legend that became accepted (*Antiquitates Judaica* I,4; 93–94 AD).

In the book illumination of the Early and High Middle Ages, local buildings that were less than monumental were used as models for the architecture of the Tower of Babel. Starring in the 16th century, artists orientated themselves on the Mesopotamian type of step-shaped ziggurat (temple tower), which, however, was rectangular rather than round. Bruegel's monumental composition had several forerunners in Netherlandish painting, but his work became the most famous classic among the Tower of Babel depictions and was frequently copied in many different variations.

The sense of scale is provided by the Flemish-style port city, which is impressively tiny in comparison to the tower. With meticulous precision and encyclopaedic interest Bruegel depicts an abundance of technical and mechanical details, from the supply of the building materials in the busy harbour to the various cranes and the scaffolding on the unfinished brick foundation. He sets the workers' dwellings into the stone outer structure, which blends elements of classical with Romanesque architecture, and they appear to be more than merely temporary. By anchoring the building on the rocky slope, Bruegel creates the impression of static equilibrium. Reaching up to the clouds, the building, however, is optically distorted and appears to have slightly sunk into the ground on the left side. This is an artistic gesture, on the one hand enhancing the impression of the building's monumentality, and on the other hand alluding to human hubris and the impossibility of completing the tower because "the Lord confused the language of all the earth". (Gen. 11:9.)

ALONSO SÁNCHEZ COELLO
(Valencia, 1531/32 –
Madrid, 1588)
1564
Canvas, 186 x 82.5 cm
Inv. No. 3235

Trained in Portugal, Alonso Sánchez Coello moved to Antwerp in 1550. He studied under Antonis Mor (Anthony More), an established court-portrait specialist who had been in the employ of the Spanish King Philip II since 1554. Sánchez Coello followed his teacher to Madrid in 1559 and assumed his position shortly after 1560.

The present portrait of Don Carlos (1545–1568), the only son of Philip II and his first wife (and cousin), Mary of Portugal, was commissioned by Emperor Maximilian II and finished in 1564. Because marriage was planned between Maximilian's daughter Anna and Don Carlos, her second cousin, the portrait was sent soon after its creation to the Vienna court. The chosen bridegroom, however, was mentally and physically handicapped. A crooked back and a shortened leg restricted his movements, and he was prone to violent outbursts of rage. A head injury resulting from a fall in 1562 had made the situation considerably worse. In 1568 his father finally ordered his arrest. The infant responded with hunger strikes, and his condition deteriorated rapidly. Four months later Don Carlos died. Rumours were spread by the political opponents of the king that he had poisoned his defiant son but these were probably just propaganda. In any case, the heroically depicted protagonist in Schiller's *Don Carlos, Infant of Spain* (1787) and Verdi's *Don Carlo* (1867) has little in common with the historical person.

The painter masterfully disguised the unfavourable physical condition of the potential bridegroom: depicted in the standardised posture characteristic of the full-length court portrait, Don Carlos is turned slightly to the side, making the different length of his legs appear balanced, and the distortion of his torso is hidden underneath the dark cape thrown over his shoulders. Viewers are kept at a distance by the cool coloration and matt surfaces.

PIETER BRUEGEL THE ELDER
(Breda?, ca. 1526/30 –
Brussels, 1569)
1565
Wood, 117 x 162 cm
Inv. No. 1838

In the late 16th century, the Antwerp banker Niclaes Jongelinck owned one of the most important painting collections in the Netherlands. He commissioned Bruegel to create a series of six seasonal paintings, the last of which is shown here. The series also included: *Gloomy Day (Early Spring)* (KHM, GG, Inv. No. 1837); *Spring* (now lost); *Hay-Harvest (Early Summer)* (Nelahozeves Castle, Czech Republic, Lobkowitz Collection); *The Harvesters (Late Summer)* (New York, Metropolitan Museum of Art); *Return of the Herd (Autumn)* (KHM, GG, Inv. No. 1018).

For the composition of this series, Bruegel, who today is regarded as the most progressive landscape painter of the 16th century, followed an older tradition that divided the year, beginning on 1 March, into six unequally long seasons. What all the compositions have in common is the so-called balcony motif, i.e., the depiction of a hill in the foreground from which an overall view of the land-scape unfolds. On top of the hill a group of hunters accompanied by a pack of dogs is seen, making their way back to the village below. Their catch is poor: a single fox dangling from the spear the hunter on the left carries on his shoulder. To the hunter's left, Bruegel added a motif that had been used for quire some time in book illumination for depicting the month of December: the preparations for singeing a pig over an open fire outside a building. The damaged sign hanging above them reveals the name of the inn: "dit is in den Hert", meaning "To the Deer" – a well-aimed passing shot. Entertaining details, such as the people ice-skating on the frozen lakes, have contributed to the painting's enormous popularity. However, it does not owe its significance in art history to its details but rather to the overall impression conveyed by the coloration and composition. With virtuosity and consistency Bruegel evokes the impression of cold: white, blue-green and brown are the dominant colours. The precise silhouette of the trees, the frozen mill-wheel at the lower right and the icy surface of the snow revealed by the hunters' footprints blend together to convey the fundamental characteristics of winter. The scene is an invented, universally formulated landscape: the combination of a chain of Alpine moun-tains with Flemish architecture renders pointless any search for reality.

51 JACOPO STRADA

TIZIANO VECELLIO,
CALLED TITIAN
(Pieve di Cadore, ca. 1488 –
Venice, 1576)
Ca. 1567/68
Canvas, 125 x 95 cm
Inv. No. 81

Jacopo Strada of Mantua (1515–1588) was a painter, architect and goldsmith and much sought after as an art expert. His primary occupation, however, was dealing in the art of antiquity. In 1553 Strada had issued a scholarly publication on his own extensive coin collection. Four years later he moved to Vienna, where he worked for the emperors Ferdinand I, Maximilian II and Rudolf II. In 1566 the title "antiquarius caesarius" was conferred upon him, and eight years later he was raised to the nobility. Strada was also in business contact with Titian.

The portrait was painted during a stay in Venice and exhibits the pastose, restless application of paint that characterised the beginning of Titian's late period. Strada is identified by his heavy golden chain as a member of the court; the sword and the fur that seems to have slipped from his right shoulder are evidence of his affluence. On the table lie a letter, coins and an antique torso. Strada himself is holding a completely preserved statuette, a Roman copy of the Aphrodite Pseliumene by Praxiteles. In the background, above his head, lie two books – perhaps Strada's own publications. The cartouche with an inscription on the right was once assumed to have been a later addition because the design appeared to be too Baroque, but the results of more recent scholarly studies speak against that assumption. Strada's posture was influenced by Moroni's portrait of the sculptor Alessandro Vittoria (Cat. No. 41) and is unique among Titian's portraits: the opposing motion of the arms and head gives it an individual dynamism and creates distance to the viewer. It remains an open question whether Titian was seeking in a subtle manner to criticise the aggressive business practices of the imperial antiquarian.

PIETER BRUEGEL THE ELDER
(Breda?, ca. 1526/30 –
Brussels, 1569)
Ca. 1568
Wood, 114 x 164 cm
Inv. No. 1027

Bruegel has created a virtuoso structure in his depiction of a peasant celebration: the long, crowded banquet table creates a diagonal on which all the figures in the composition are oriented. From outside, where it is still daylight, other guests are pressing into the room. One of the bagpipe-players draws our attention to the front, where he looks with curiosity at the meagre fare that is being freshly served. Two helpers are using a door that has been taken off its hinges to carry their dishes. A server who is pouring beer into more easily handled jugs and a child eating to one side close off the painting at the front. If we follow the figure at the end of the table who is passing the dishes to the wedding guests, we are led to the true protagonist, the bride. She is sitting silently in front of a length of green cloth, which has been hung along with a paper crown in her honour on the straw wall. According to Flemish custom, the bridegroom was not allowed to attend the celebrations until the evening, and the bride was not permitted either to eat or to speak beforehand.

Unfortunately nothing is known about the commissioning of this work, which is probably Bruegel's most famous. If we knew more, it might help to resolve the controversial question of whether the painting is intended to be a caricature or carry a moralising message. Bruegel scholars in Vienna agree, however, that most of the interpretative proposals made thus far have failed to reveal the true meaning of the painting. Attempts have been made, for example, to connect the large shoes with the German expression "auf großem Fuß leben" (to live in great style) or to see the two-piece bride's crown as an indication that she is pregnant. It is far more in keeping with Bruegel's humanistic conception of himself to see the painting as a neutral observation without further intent. The choice of the subject was nothing decisively new in Netherlands graphic art and painting, but never before had it been taken up with such compositional and motivic density and from such a benevolent distance.

53 NYMPH AND SHEPHERD

TIZIANO VECELLIO,
CALLED TITIAN
(Pieve di Cadore, ca. 1488 –
Venice, 1576)
Ca. 1570/75
Canvas, 149.6 x 187 cm
Inv. No. 1825

Blurred outlines that take shape only when viewed from a certain distance, particularly with regards to the motifs in the background, and a colour range fogged by a veil of grey are characteristic of Titian's late period. The present painting, which is one of the artist's last works, does not depict a specific scene taken from mythology or literature; its type is the pastoral, which evolved in Venetian art starring in 1500.

A "shepherd", ready to begin playing his flute, has approached the female figure from behind as she rests in the shade of a tree. He turns towards her while she looks over her right shoulder, equivocally smiling at the viewer. The "nymph" is reclining on a panther skin, which along with the goat climbing a barren tree-stump in the background symbolises lust. In the work of other artists as well, the reclining nude seen from the rear is often connected with depictions of Venus. Although the goddess does not set the theme, she adds another aspect of love to the Arcadian scene. Here painting demonstrates its potential to rival poetry. As in the early 16th century (cf. Cat. No. 19), the content is provided by the lyric poetry of the early modern era influenced by Petrarch: its fundamental motif is the desire for an ideal love affair that ultimately cannot be realised.

54   MAN WITH A WHITE BEARD

JACOPO ROBUSTI,
CALLED TINTORETTO
(Venice, 1518 –
Venice, 1594)
Ca. 1570/78
Canvas, 92.4 x 59.5 cm
Inv. No. 25

The unknown subject looks directly at the viewer. Dressed in a coat that almost entirely disappears into the darkness of the background, he holds the fur trimming with his left hand to keep the coat closed. Tintoretto uses this trick to distance the subject from the viewer despite the direct eye contact. He gives the man's skin a tone that corresponds with his dark-red shirt and emphasises the varied structure and quality of his hair and beard. With simple compositional means and striking illumination, Tintoretto gives his aged subject a strong presence, individuality and "spiritual beauty", a quality that is increasingly found in Tintoretto's late portraits. Contrary to long-held assumptions, the painting is now ascribed to Tintoretto himself and no longer to his son Domenico. It owes its popularity in Austria not least to the role it played as a persistently recurring motif in Thomas Bernhard's comedy *Alte Meister* (1985) (*Old Masters,* 1989).

55   HERCULES, DEIANIRA AND THE CENTAUR NESSUS

BARTHOLOMÄUS SPRANGER
(Antwerp, 1546 –
Prague, 1611)
Soon after 1580
Canvas, 112 x 82 cm
Inv. No. 2613

Apart from Hans von Aachen (Cat. No. 57), it was primarily the Netherlandish artist Bartholomäus Spranger who dominated the art of painting at the court of Emperor Rudolf II. Spranger had spent ten years (1565–1575) in Milan, Parma and Rome before coming to Prague in 1580. The present painting was one of his first imperial commissions and probably part of a series of mythological depictions. Spranger reduced the dramatic action to an obvious arrangement of the participating characters set against an almost neutral background. The powerful physiognomy of the figures and their twisted postures reflect the influence of sculptors such as Giambologna and Adriaen de Vries.

On the way to their home, Hercules and Deianira reach the river Evenus, which is in flood. The Centaur Nessus offers to help the newlyweds cross the river. While Hercules can easily master the floods on his own, Nessus is supposed to carry the weaker Deianira to the other side. Too late does Hercules realise that Nessus wants to abduct and seduce his wife; he can save her only by shooting the traitor. As he lies dying, however, the Centaur – depicted with extreme foreshortening at the bottom left corner of the painting – sets the stage for his deadly revenge: he tells Deianira that his blood holds the power of love. If ever in need, she should dip a piece of cloth into it (which can be seen here between the lovers, foreboding Hercules's fate), sew Hercules a tunic from it, and give it to him as a present. When Deianira makes use of it in despair a few years later, the cloth, which contrary to the Centaur's promise has been soaked in poison, clings to Hercules's body, setting his flesh afire. He chooses to commit suicide, immolating himself on a pyre, and Deianira follows him into death. The erotic allusions are obvious: Amor appears at the upper left of the painting as the figure responsible for their sorrow and looks ironically at the doomed couple.

PAOLO CALIARI,
CALLED VERONESE
(Verona, 1528 –
Venice, 1588)
Ca. 1582
Canvas, 111 x 100.5 cm
Inv. No. 34

Only in his late works did Veronese begin to use darker coloration and depict restless, emotional figures, as seen in the present painting. In the early 1580s he worked on the decoration of the Sala del Consiglio dei Dieci (Hall of the Council of Ten) at the Doge's Palace in Venice. This half-length portrait of the heroine was probably also created during this period.

To sum up the story from the Old Testament: during the siege of the city of Bethulia by the Assyrians, Judith succeeded through her courage and cunning in entering the camp of the general Holofernes and beheading him in his sleep, thus giving her people victory over the now-leaderless Assyrian troops.

Veronese depicts the moment when Judith is about to hand her victim's severed head to the servant standing to her right. Although the heroine is clad in orange-red and blue-coloured garments adorned with precious jewellery, there is nothing openly triumphant in her gestures. Melancholy and yet in command of the situation, Judith accepts her deed. Tenderly, but perhaps also a bit reluctantly, she reaches for the head of Holofernes. She averts her gaze from him and looks at the servant, who, however, stares at the horrifying object in front of her. Veronese has placed the head in dose proximity to the viewer and even suggests that Judith is about to remove it from view in a sweeping movement.

The uncertain provenance of the work and the supposition that it has been cut down make it difficult to determine its original use. It possibly belonged to a series of *donne famose,* depictions of famous, heroic women (also cf. Veronese's *Lucretia;* KHM, GG, Inv. No. 1561).

57   BACCHUS, CERES AND AMOR (?)

HANS VON AACHEN
(Cologne, 1552 –
Prague, 1615)
Ca. 1600
Canvas, 163 x 113 cm
Inv. No. 1098

Born in the Rhineland but trained by a Netherlandish master in Cologne, Hans von Aachen was the most important painter at the Prague court, apart from Bartholomäus Spranger (Cat. No. 55). Like his rival, Aachen had spent a long time in Italy (Venice, Rome and Florence, ca. 1574 – 1587/88). Characteristic of both are the combination of Netherlandish surface treatment and the Mannerist proportions and postures of the figures, which date back to Parmigianino (cf. Cat. Nos. 27, 34). Thus both artists are regarded as exponents of one of the last manifestations of European Mannerism. It finds its expression here in explicitly courtly features, which were personally advocated by Emperor Rudolf II. The clear preference for erotic subjects is also a distinctive feature of Rudolfine court art.

Ceres, the Roman goddess of fertility, dominates the foreground of the painting in a striking rear view. Her elongated limbs and the opposing movements of her torso and head are characteristic features of Mannerism. Bacchus, the god of wine, has approached Ceres from behind. He tenderly touches her, looking at her in joyful anticipation, while she fixes her gaze on the viewer. The boy at the bottom left presents them with a basket of fruit and vegetables. Although the figure of the child has not been clearly identified as Amor, this interpretation would make sense: "Sine Cerere et Baccho friget Venus" – "Without Ceres and Bacchus, Venus is cold" (or figuratively: "Without food and drink, love cools"). This quotation from the Roman dramatist Terence (ca. 190 – 159 BC) has become a proverbial phrase and is probably the key to understanding this emblematic picture. The "freezing" Venus, traditionally warming her hands by a fire, is missing. It is possible, however, that the narrow streak of light at the top left corner in the back, standing out against the stony background, is the reflection of this fire.

MICHELANGELO MERISI,
CALLED CARAVAGGIO
(Milan, 1571 –
Port'Ercole, 1610)
Ca. 1601/05
Canvas, 364.5 x 249.5 cm
Inv. No. 147

So far, no one has succeeded in reconstructing the exact history of how this altar painting came about, either because essential documents were missing or existing documents provided contradictory information. Thus the donor seeking protection at St. Dominic's elbow at the left edge of the painting remains unidentified. According to the latest research, the picture was painted in Naples rather than in Rome and thus in the period between 1601 and 1605. Its existence is first documented in 1607, when it was already being put up for sale in Naples. The owners, two Dutch art dealers, returned to Amsterdam with the painting sometime before 1617. There it was acquired in 1618/19 by an Antwerp consortium, to which Rubens and Jan Brueghel the Elder belonged, before it finally found a new home in Antwerp's Dominican Church. In 1781 the *Madonna of the Rosary* was acquired for the imperial collection of paintings at the instigation of Emperor Joseph II.

Pope Gregory XIII instituted the Feast of the Holy Rosary in 1573, following the victory of the allied Christian forces over the Turkish fleet at Lepanto (1571), and entrusted the Dominican order with its observance. St. Peter Martyr, who can be recognised by his wounded head, turns as holy mediator towards the viewer. He indicates to the faithful the presence of the enthroned Madonna with the child Jesus. She, on the other hand, turns to the side, ordering St. Dominic, who is looking up in obedience, to distribute rosaries to the people who are pressing towards him on their knees. But ultimately even Mary plays only the role of a mediator – the boy Jesus is the focus of attention with regards to both content and composition. As in most of his works, Caravaggio achieves the strong physical presence of the figures in a realistic, never idealising manner through the use of intense contrasts of light and dark. He subtly makes the objects of their desire, the rosaries, more abstract by putting them in the shadows, making the brightly illuminated hands all the more dominant.

59   THE CROWNING WITH THORNS

MICHELANGELO MERISI,
CALLED CARAVAGGIO
(Milan, 1571 –
Port'Ercole, 1610)
Ca. 1602/05
Canvas, 127 x 165.5 cm
Inv. No. 307

Only in recent years has the prominent origin of this work, which was acquired in 1810 by the imperial ambassador in Rome, been clear: it came from the collection of Vincenzo Giustiniani, who in around 1600 had begun compiling in Rome what was to become one of the most influential collections of European Baroque art. In addition to hundreds of works of ancient sculpture, the collection included fifteen pictures by Caravaggio alone, among them *The Crowning with Thorns*. It is mentioned in the collection inventory as a *supraporte,* a painting destined to be hung over a doorway, and indeed the half-length composition is painted with slight foreshortening.

Caravaggio's interest in the sculpture of antiquity, which he developed particularly during his stay in Rome in the period before 1606, is evident in the bent posture of Christ. There is a relationship with a particular model: the *Belvedere Torso,* which was mentioned for the first time in the 15th century and went on display at the Vatican sometime around 1530. With a complete command of anatomy, Caravaggio characterises the varied physical appearance of the protagonists. Christ's delicate skin is in obvious contrast to the bronzed appearance of his tormentors. His exposed, outstretched neck, which has been forced into a horizontal position, is a clear indication of the brutality of the action. Caravaggio uses decisive contrasts of light and dark to create a strong physical presence. Remarkable is his use of so-called incision, in which he used a sharp instrument to outline the principal contours of his composition on the surface before he began painting. It is not clear whether he did this free-hand or with the help of a pattern drawn on paper.

JAN BRUEGHEL THE ELDER
(Brussels, 1568 –
Antwerp, 1625)
1606/07
Wood, 98 x 73 cm
Inv. No. 570

"[…] when winter approaches, covering everything in ice, I take pleasure in the view – and in my imagination even in the scent – of flowers, if not real ones then the artificial kind found in the painting." In 1606 Jan Brueghel the Elder, the son of Pieter Bruegel the Elder (Cat. Nos. 46, 48, 50, 52), painted the earliest of his surviving still lifes of flowers (Milan, Pinacoteca Ambrosiana) for the author of the above words, the archbishop of Milan, Federigo Borromeo (1564–1631). The painter spent many years in Italy and remembered to the end of his life the fruitful patronage of this important collector, who also founded the Ambrosiana.

Flowers in a Wooden Vessel was painted for Archduke Albert VII, the sovereign regent of the Spanish Netherlands, and became one of the most famous floral still lifes in European art. The grand format, the perfect painting technique and the highly successful composition make it a characteristic piece for an art collection of the time. However, the references usually found in floral still lifes to the transitoriness of all earthly things occur only incidentally: a few of the flowers that have fallen are wilted or have been damaged by insects. The artist has disregarded the fact that the plants included in his painting flower at various times of the year. Here they all bloom at once, a situation otherwise found only in the "eternal spring" of paradise. In a letter written to Milan in 1608, Brueghel noted that such flowers would be "far too costly" to "have them at home. […] Thus I was in Brussels to paint several flowers […] from life". Creating a legend, he suggests that his still lifes were not only based on real plants but in some cases even painted outdoors. This, however, would not have been permitted by the technical demands of oil painting; more likely Brueghel was working from graphic reproductions created during the new revival of botany. Thus his description of his method is in keeping with the "artistically staged naturalness" that contemporary art theory expected of a floral still life.

145

61 CHRIST ON THE MOUNT OF OLIVES (CHRIST'S FEAR OF DEATH)

GIOVANNI BATTISTA
CARACCIOLO,
CALLED BATTISTELLO
(Naples, 1578 –
Naples, 1635)
Ca. 1615
Canvas, 148 x 124 cm
Inv. No. F 17

"And there appeared an angel unto him from heaven, strengthening him. And being in an agony he prayed more earnestly: and his sweat was as it were great drops of blood falling down to the ground." (Luke 22:43–44.)

Unlike many of his Neapolitan contemporaries, Caracciolo early oriented himself on the modern lighting effects and the close proximity of the compositions in the works of Caravaggio (Cat. Nos. 58, 59), becoming the latter's most important successor in Naples. At the same time, however, Caracciolo also adopted the demand for the representation and severity of the contemporary Roman art that evolved around Annibale and Lodovico Carracci.

In this characteristic early work Caracciolo complies with the demands of the Counter-Reformation for a literal account of the biblical tale of Christ's fear of death while creating a carefully calculated mood for the devout beholder. Caracciolo gives Christ the features of the Ecce Homo: his hands are folded across his chest, and his eyelids are contorted. With a moving physical closeness the comforting figure of the angel turns towards him. The severity of the composition and the abstract effect of the body surfaces emphasise the urgency of the appeal.

In the 1659 inventory of Archduke Leopold Wilhelm's gallery, the painting was attributed to Caravaggio himself out of ignorance of the true author. It has been listed under the name of Caracciolo only since 1962.

147

62 THE MIRACLES OF ST. FRANCIS XAVIER, *MODELLO*

PETER PAUL RUBENS
(Siegen, 1577 –
Antwerp, 1640)
Ca. 1617
Wood, 104.5 x 72.5 cm
Inv. No. 528

Construction of the new Jesuit Church in Antwerp began in 1615, and Rubens received a commission to provide ceiling paintings (lost in a fire) for the aisles and galleries as well as two high-altar paintings. The images of the two altarpieces, like theatre scenery, had to be changeable in accordance with the church year, and thus a complicated mechanism was required. Franciscus Aguilonius, rector of the Jesuit Seminary since 1613, wanted to promote the canonisation of the founder of the Jesuit Order, Ignatius of Loyola (KHM, GG, Inv. Nos. 530 and 517), and Francis Xavier with monumental altarpieces.

It was traditional workshop procedure for Rubens to first create a *modello.* This small-format version served as a model for further co-ordination with the client and was the basis for the execution of the large-format painting by Rubens and his studio.

In 1541 Francis Xavier was sent to Eastern India, Malacca, Ceylon, Japan and Singapore to perform missionary work. He is depicted in the present sketch in front of a partly fascinated, partly sceptical audience, some of them dressed in seemingly oriental clothing. A blind man is standing to the right of the protagonist's feet, while people who have been brought back from the dead can be seen to his left. A heathen temple with falling idols dominates the background. Rubens combined these pictorial images in a flowing, exciting and mature composition in the *modello,* but the differences between the sketch and the large-format painting (Cat. No. 63) are nonetheless interesting. With the aim of making the composition more legible when viewed from a distance, Rubens made several changes, most of them regarding the protagonist. In the finished painting Francis Xavier occupies a more isolated and thus more powerful position. Another interesting detail is the mother holding her lifeless child in her arms at the left edge of the sketch. In the painting Rubens depicted the infant in prone position with water running from its mouth, thus making its death by drowning clear to the viewer.

63   THE MIRACLES OF ST. FRANCIS XAVIER

PETER PAUL RUBENS
(Siegen, 1577 –
Antwerp, 1640)
Ca. 1617/18
Canvas, 535 x 395 cm
Inv. No. 519

Like a monument, the protagonist stands in a dark robe with deep folds on the plinth-like projection of a wall. Francis Xavier dominates the scene as the "missionary to the Asian peoples", his left hand pointing to Fides, the personification of faith, his right hand extended towards the toppling idols, and his gaze turned to the listeners and supplicants.

Rubens has used dramatic lighting – the Jesuit is back-lit – to stage the group of listeners and observers, who, keeping a respectful distance, are bathed in bright light. Standing in the shadows the armoured soldier creates an optical turning point in the composition, leading the gaze of the viewer to the actual miracle depicted: in the left foreground deathly pale figures are rising from their graves. The blind man on the right, whose striking posture is based on a work by Raphael, provides counterbalance in the composition. His outstretched arms also strengthen the compositional effect of the "plinth" on which Francis Xavier is standing.

It was hoped that placing the work on the high altar of the new church in 1618 would hasten the canonisation of Francis Xavier, and indeed both he and the founder of the Jesuits, Ignatius of Loyola, were canonised in 1622. In addition to the *modello* (Cat. No. 62), the altarpiece was preceded by a large number of drawings of the individual elements. Most of the execution of the monumental altarpiece, which was designed to be viewed from a distance and create maximum effect in the church, was carried out by members of Rubens's studio with the great painter himself only reworking important features. But the concept and thus the most important aspect of the work was entirely by Rubens.

For the previous history of the painting cf. Cat. No. 62.

64 HERO MOURNING THE DEAD LEANDER

DOMENICO FETTI
(Rome [?], ca. 1588/89 –
Venice, 1623)
Ca. 1621/22
Wood, 41 x 97 cm
Inv. No. 160

Unconventionally and without direct succession, Fetti dismantles the colours into contrasting shades. The result is an unreal and abstract compositional space. His characteristic painting style breaks away from the outlines and is flooded with light. Thus Fetti partly anticipated the achievements of the late-Baroque Venetian painters (among them, Guardi, Cat. No. 100).

During a celebration in honour of Aphrodite, Leander became enamoured of Hero, who, however, had devoted her life to serving the goddess of love as a priestess. Thus they had to keep their love secret. Leander, who lived in Abydos on the other side of the Hellespont (today's Dardanelles), swam across the dangerous strait every night, guided by a light that Hero put in the window of her tower. When a storm extinguished the fire one night, the youth lost his bearings and drowned. Hero found his corpse washed ashore the following morning, and in despair she flung herself from her tower into the sea. The scene of Hero mourning her lover is moved into the foreground, while Fetti depicts the tragic fate of the heroine on the right.

Domenico Fetti was court painter to Duke Ferdinando Gonzaga of Mantua, who had probably met the artist in Rome. In 1621 at the latest, the painter travelled to Venice for the second time. Upon his return he fell out with the Gonzaga, and Fetti moved back to Venice, never to return to Mantua. Along with two other works (KHM, GG, Inv. Nos. 172, 7722), the present painting was among the last by the artist, who died prematurely. It is possible that this series was commissioned by a Venetian client and conceived as decoration for a piece of furniture or wall panelling.

65   THE BAPTISM OF CHRIST

GUIDO RENI
(Calvenzano, 1575 –
Bologna, 1642)
Ca. 1622/23
Canvas, 263.5 x 186.5 cm
Inv. No. 222

Guido Reni received his first training in Bologna in the studio of the Carracci family of painters, who were at the opposite artistic pole from Caravaggio (cf. Cat. Nos. 58, 59). While not averse to innovation, they rather adhered to classic Renaissance figural ideals and promoted the further development of the Baroque from this standpoint. In 1622, after spending time in Rome, Ravenna and Naples, Reni took over the workshop of his teachers, becoming Bologna's leading painter.

The Baptism of Christ was commissioned by the Flemish silversmith Jan Jacobs. Before it was even finished, it was taken to the Netherlands in 1623 and then sold to an English buyer several years later (before 1628). In 1649 it was acquired from the collection of the Duke of Buckingham for the imperial collection in Prague.

Reni's depiction of this key event is presented in a calm and balanced manner, with gentle light, reverent gestures and a discreet lack of direct eye contact. At first glance, there is little to distinguish the appearance of the two protagonists from one another. The body of St. John the Baptist is darker, while Christ is depicted in the moment of his baptism as humble and gentle. The Dove of the Holy Spirit and the beam of light emanating from it repeat the diagonal of the cross that St. John is holding in his left hand and focus complete attention on the baptismal act. Reni elegantly veils the rock on which St. John's knee is resting – it makes hardly any visual impression at all. The glowing red garment at the centre may be an allusion to the Passion of Christ.

66 LANDSCAPE WITH PHILEMON AND BAUCIS

PETER PAUL RUBENS
(Siegen, 1577 –
Antwerp, 1640)
Ca. 1625
Wood, 146 x 208.5 cm
Inv. No. 690

Having originally planned only a stormy landscape, Rubens – as so often – expanded the composition in the process of the painting's creation and added a mythological staffage of human and divine figures to the pure landscape. This is firmly in keeping with Flemish tradition, which, unlike the Netherlandish one, almost always enhanced landscapes with Christian or mythological narratives.

On a forest path slightly ascending from the centre to the right, four figures appear: two elderly people, arduously propped up on walking sticks and accompanied by two gods, have escaped the storm still raging at the centre of the painting. They are Philemon and Baucis. Shortly before the storm, they were the only ones to give shelter, food and drink to the gods, who were travelling through the land disguised as weary travellers. The punishment for the hard-heartedness of the other people was swift to follow – Jupiter and Mercury showed only this married couple the way to the safety of a hill in time (Ovid, *Metamorphoses* 8:620–720). In the foreground the effects of the forces of nature are drastically depicted: helplessly, an ox lies trapped in a broken tree above the torrential floods; on the left, near the rainbow, the corpses of a mother and her child have been washed ashore; above them a man fortunate enough to have escaped clings to a tree that is still standing.

The present *Landscape with Philemon and Baucis* was probably painted entirely by Rubens himself, without the help of his workshop. Like most of his landscapes it was not a commissioned piece. This subject is rare in painting: since the 16th century depictions of the myth have mostly shown Philemon and Baucis playing host to the gods in their home.

67 NICOLAS LANIER

ANTON VAN DYCK
(Antwerp, 1599 –
London, 1641)
1628
Canvas, 111 x 87.6 cm
Inv. No. 501

Nicolas Lanier (1588–1666) had been court musical director to Charles I since 1625 and was one of the agents the English king sent to Mantua in order to monitor the transport to London of the ducal collection he had acquired a short time earlier. The precious cargo was first brought to Antwerp, where the present portrait was probably painted. According to contemporary sources, Lanier spent seven days in van Dyck's studio, sitting for the Flemish painter, who had returned from Italy only a short time earlier (1627). They possibly knew one another from van Dyck's first short stay in England (1620/21).

Lanier, his right arm self-confidently placed akimbo, is clad in silken courtly attire. Covering his left shoulder and upper body, the black fabric of his cloak creates an impressive contrast to the red and white colour of his shirt; his right hand is hidden beneath it, while his left rests on the hilt of his sword. The narrow vista of an idyllic landscape extends the image towards the back.

Lanier's posture and expression are in keeping with *sprezzatura,* the "elegant nonchalance" typical of the ideal courtier, described by Baldassare Castiglione in his *Book of the Courtier (Il Libro del Cortegiano,* 1528) and especially cultivated at the Stuart court. In addition, van Dyck adopted a classical compositional type from Titian. He probably did so in the knowledge that Lanier would give the picture to the English king, who with the ducal collection of Mantua had just acquired one of the finest collections of Venetian paintings. Van Dyck's tribute to Titian probably resulted in his being summoned again to the English court in 1632, where he would create a new type of English noble portrait that has retained its effectiveness to this day.

159

68 THE VISION OF THE BLESSED HERMANN JOSEPH

ANTON VAN DYCK
(Antwerp, 1599 –
London, 1641)
1629/30
Canvas, 160 x 128 cm
Inv. No. 488

After spending several years in Italy, where he acquired a refined knowledge of Venetian painting, Anthony van Dyck returned to Antwerp in 1627. He joined the Jesuit Confraternity of Bachelors and in 1630 was appointed – as Rubens had been decades earlier – court painter to Isabella Clara Eugenia, the regent of the Spanish Netherlands. During this period he created two altarpieces for the brotherhood: *Madonna and Child Enthroned with Saints Rosalia, Peter and Paul* (KHM, GG, Inv. No. 482) in 1629, and, immediately afterwards, this slightly smaller painting. The legend of the Premonstratensian monk Hermann Joseph (ca. 1200) was probably chosen as the subject for the altarpiece because the head of the brotherhood at the time shared his name. The monk's vision of his marriage to the Madonna was the pinnacle of his pronounced worship of the Virgin Mary. Deep affection, devotion and emotion mark the posture, gestures and face of the kneeling monk, while the Madonna appears distant, superior and cool. The smiling angel, with his right arm and shoulder exposed, takes on the role of the mediator both with regards to composition and content. All emotions seem to be concentrated in his billowing robe. Helpfully, he has taken the monk's hand and is gently leading it towards the Madonna's fingertips. In comparison to similar compositions by Rubens, who was 22 years older and in whose studio van Dyck had worked in his youth, the younger painter emphasises the aspects of emotion mainly with gentle movements, using soft, broken coloration; thus the emotional interaction between the protagonists gains in importance.

The suggestion that the figure at the left edge of the picture is a self-portrait of van Dyck remains unproven. In any case, he was no longer so youthful when the painting was executed. The painter left Antwerp in 1632 and worked as court painter to the English king in London until his death in 1641.

69 SAMSON AND DELILAH

ANTON VAN DYCK
(Antwerp, 1599 –
London, 1641)
Ca. 1630
Canvas, 146 x 254 cm
Inv. No. 512

While fleeing from the Philistines, Samson fell in love with Delilah. This did not go unnoticed by his pursuers, and they promised Delilah a large amount of silver if she could find out wherein his great strength lay. Upon her questioning, he lied to her three times and his capture failed, but Delilah did not give up, reminding him that their love vow did not permit secrets. Finally, he told her the truth and revealed the connection between his power and his hair. "And she made him sleep upon her knees […] and she called for a man, and she caused him to shave off the seven locks of his head. […] and his strength went from him. […] And he awoke […] and said, I will go out as at other times before, and shake myself. And he wist not that the LORD was departed from him. But the Philistines took him, and put out his eyes, and brought him down to Gaza […] and he did grind in the prison house." (Judges 16:19–21.)

Van Dyck used several artistic sources for the present painting: one detail of the scene – Samson's desperately grasping the leg of the traitress – is borrowed from a work by Titian. With this adaptation van Dyck introduced a significant change of interpretation that became characteristic of his work, although it derives from Rubens with regard to its landscape format and the diagonal depiction of Samson's gestures. Delilah's dismay at betraying her lover is mingled with grief over her loss. She seems to regret her treacherous act, or at least is painfully moved by its dramatic consequence. Van Dyck "sentimentalises" the event, while Rubens had portrayed Delilah as an unscrupulous seductress and Samson as a captive, entirely occupied with fending off the soldiers.

PETER PAUL RUBENS
(Siegen, 1577 –
Antwerp, 1640)
1630/32
Wood,
centre panel: 352 x 236 cm,
side wings: 352 x 109 cm each
Inv. No. 678

In 1588 the brother of Emperor Rudolf II and viceroy of Portugal, Albert VII, founded the St. Ildefonso Brotherhood in Lisbon. Following the appointment of Albert and his wife Isabella (a daughter of the Spanish King Philip II) as sovereign regents of the Spanish Netherlands, he moved the headquarters of the brotherhood to Brussels in 1603. This explains why a saint seldom revered in Flanders found his way into one of the most significant altarpieces of Rubens's late period. The infanta commissioned the work in Albert's memory in 1630, nine years after his death.

According to legend, while walking through his church one day, the Spanish monk (605–667; 657 archbishop of Toledo) was surprised by a blazing light and the vision of the Virgin Mary on a throne, accompanied by two female saints. While his companions took flight, he approached the venerated saint and was presented with a precious chasuble she had made herself. The donors appear on the wings of the altar in the company of their patron saints.

Rubens had not used the form of the triptych since 1618. Why the painter and client chose this antiquated type more than a decade later remains unclear. Perhaps the depiction of the donor and her (by then deceased) husband to the right and left of the central panel was an attempt to circumvent an order issued in 1608, which – although not always obeyed – forbade the use of portraits of living people in the central altar panel. The wings, however, are so closely tied to the centre panel with regards to composition that the physical division of the three sections by the frame is of hardly any consequence: the red of the velvet draped over the two prie-dieux returns in the garment of the Virgin Mary, while the yellow-gold colour of the regents' attire is reflected in the niche behind the throne. Conversely, the dark robes of the patron saints form atonal unity with the habit of the male protagonist. The distinctive feature of this monumental work is that every part of it is in Rubens's own hand. This, however, does not apply to the outer side panels (*The Holy Family Beneath an Apple Tree;* KHM, GG, Inv. No. 698), which have also been preserved but are now separated from the original triptych.

71 ALLEGORY OF VANITY

ANTONIO DE PEREDA
(Valladolid, ca. 1611 –
Madrid, 1678)
Ca. 1634
Canvas, 139.5 x 174 cm
Inv. No. 771

We know little about the career of Antonio de Pereda, apart from the fact that he received his training in Madrid. The dear influence of Netherlandish painting is characteristic of his work, and this is particularly true of the present *Allegory*. It occupies a special place in the art of Madrid, because with it Pereda introduced to Spanish painting motifs of vanity symbolism long established in Netherlandish art: the brilliant and subtly differentiated depiction of skulls, a blown-out candle, an hourglass (to its left the line "Nil omne" – "All is nothing") and brittle folios. Pereda arranges these items together with precious pieces of armour and a firearm on a bare wooden surface. Time, happiness, wartime fame, beauty and science are the exposed attributes of vanity, which the winged Genius on the far side of the composition presents to the viewer: a precious clock, miniature portraits with a string of pearls (documents of a happy marriage?) and a handful of coins. In his left hand the Genius holds a cameo with the portrait of Emperor Charles V (1500–1558), while his right hand points to a globe, alluding to the world domination of the Casa de Austria.

All the above-mentioned details suggest that the painting was a courtly commission. This is all the more likely as we know that Pereda participated in the painterly decoration of the Salón de Reinos in Madrid's Buen Retiro palace in the early 1630s and thus worked for Spain's King Philip IV.

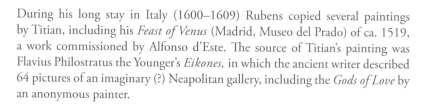

PETER PAUL RUBENS
(Siegen, 1577 –
Antwerp, 1640)
Ca. 1636/37
Canvas, 217 x 350 cm
Inv. No. 684

During his long stay in Italy (1600–1609) Rubens copied several paintings by Titian, including his *Feast of Venus* (Madrid, Museo del Prado) of ca. 1519, a work commissioned by Alfonso d'Este. The source of Titian's painting was Flavius Philostratus the Younger's *Eikones,* in which the ancient writer described 64 pictures of an imaginary (?) Neapolitan gallery, including the *Gods of Love* by an anonymous painter.

Twenty years after his study of the Italian model, Rubens began a painting on the same subject but expanded the repertoire of figures in his dynamic composition. Venus, the goddess of love, is the centre of attention. The posture of her arms is in keeping with the classical type of the Venus Pudica, which is characterised by its ambivalence: bashful concealment can also become its opposite – the effect on the viewer remains open. Elevated to monumental status, Venus is surrounded by numerous cupids, dancing and caressing each other and creating an appropriate setting for the feast in the tree-tops above her. Four women devote themselves to the marble cult figure: Venus is being washed, the smell of incense fills the summery air, and, finally, a precious mirror is raised to the goddess.

The group around Bacchus, the god of wine, on the left in the foreground as well as the procession of Satyrs and Maenads on the right at the back are embellishments by Rubens. In addition, the Flemish painter documented for educated contemporary viewers his knowledge of the latest results of archaeological research: the model for the round temple depicted on the left in the back and the find of a classical three-legged pot – which Rubens uses for the incense sacrifice – became known only a short time before the painting was created.

PETER PAUL RUBENS
(Siegen, 1577 –
Antwerp, 1640)
Ca. 1636/38
Wood, 176 x 83 cm
Inv. No. 688

"[…] I decided to get married because I was not yet ready to live in the renunciation that is celibacy. […] I took a wife from a good but bourgeois family, although the whole world tried to convince me to marry a lady of the court. But I feared the pride, the plague of nobility […], and thus I liked the idea of taking a wife who does not blush when she sees me pick up a brush." (Rubens in a letter to his friend Nicolas-Claude Fabri de Peiresc.) In December 1630, the 53-year-old Rubens married the 16-year-old daughter of the Antwerp silk merchant Daniel Fourment. Even Rubens's closest friends did not refrain from alluding to the great age difference between the bride and groom. His first wife, Isabella Brandt, had died of the plague in 1626. The traditional title of the painting, "her pelzken" ("The Little Fur"), comes from Rubens himself, who bequeathed the work to his young wife as a private gift. She never sold the painting; it was inherited by her children and is not documented in the inventory of the Picture Gallery before 1730.

Helena's sensual body is covered only partially by a dark fur robe, which is depicted in all its beauty. She seems to be stepping slightly to the left, while her torso remains at rest. The posture of her arms is no coincidence: it resembles the classical type of the Venus Pudica – bashful concealment or coquettish suggestion – the effect remains open. The red of the fabric on which she is standing corresponds gently with her slightly pink skin to intensify again in her reddened cheeks and sensual lips. Thus Rubens goes beyond the pure portrait genre: the image of Venus, the goddess of love and beauty, resonates in the painting. In addition he is quoting from the work of a great colleague: shortly before the creation of the present painting, Rubens had the opportunity to see Titian's *Girl in a Fur* (Cat. No. 35) in the collection of the English king and copy it. There, the charming contrast between the fair, soft skin and the dark, velvety fur had been celebrated once before.

171

NICOLAS POUSSIN
(Villers near Les Andelys,
1594 – Rome, 1665)
1638
Canvas, 148 x 199 cm
Inv. No. 1556

During the Jewish revolt against Rome (66 – 70 AD), which went down in history as the Jewish War, Flavius Josephus initially served as military commander of Galilee before being captured in 67 AD and changing sides. As advisor to the Roman troops during the siege of Jerusalem (70 AD), he tried in vain to prevent the plundering and destruction of the Temple. Even Titus, the Roman commander and son of the emperor, could not stop his troops from doing so. Flavius Josephus later (75 – 79 AD) wrote a seven-volume history of the Jewish War *(De bello Judaico)* on which this depiction is based.

Poussin came to Rome in 1624, and only a short stay in Paris (1640–1642) was to interrupt his Roman career. As a friend of his successful fellow-painter Claude Lorrain and a protégé of Pope Urban VIII and the cultured members of the papal court, Poussin became one of Rome's most prominent painters. His frequently documented interest in the art of antiquity gave his works a classical touch, which manifests itself in the present painting in its relief-like composition and plain coloration. The chaotic action appears well-organised, with the bodies precisely laid out on the canvas, and the mighty columns of the temple and the rigid figures in the foreground providing a counterweight to the battlefield tumult.

The picture was created on a commission from Cardinal Francesco Barberini and presented by an imperial envoy to Emperor Ferdinand III as a gift from the Pope in 1639. It remains uncertain what the Pope hoped to achieve in choosing the subject: was it an admonishing reminder of the conquest and plundering of Mantua by imperial troops in 1627? Or was it late praise? Ferdinand had won a decisive victory over the Protestants at the Battle of Nördlingen in 1634.

75 SELF-PORTRAIT

PETER PAUL RUBENS
(Siegen, 1577 –
Antwerp, 1640)
Ca. 1638/40
Canvas, 109.5 x 85 cm
Inv. No. 527

For this late self-portrait, which Rubens is believed to have completed in the last year of his life, he chose to portray himself not in the half-length style usual in private portraits but in an imposing view from the knees up. The massive column in the shadows (also a reference to the artist's Stoic ideals, which have often been documented), the leather gloves and the left hand resting on a sword: these are all attributes of a courtly portrait. The composition is dominated by dark tones; the only bright accents are the slightly reddish face, the pleated collar and the left hand. A powerful curve leads from Rubens's right hand across his body and left shoulder to the large dark collar, which extends almost threateningly far beyond the line of his back. Rubens concentrates most of the light in the dark-grey background. His wide-brimmed hat finally provides a compositional counterweight and closes off the painting at the top.

Although Rubens had been raised to the nobility by the Spanish monarch and knighted by the king of England, his decision to depict himself as a member of the aristocracy is nonetheless surprising: he had repeatedly distanced himself from life at court. In the final years of his life, he had largely freed himself from the responsibilities of a man of the court and diplomat, dividing his time between his city residence in Antwerp and his country castle near Elewijt. Due to serious attacks of gout, he was sometimes unable to perform even the simplest tasks. His sensitive face reflects something of his bodily ills but also the serenity of the 62-year-old artist. The fact that he painted one of the most sensual portraits of his young wife, Helena Fourment (Cat. No. 73), at about the same time adds a not unimportant aspect to our understanding of the artist's personal situation at the time.

BERNARDO CAVALLINO
(Naples, 1616 –
Naples, 1656)
Ca. 1640
Canvas, 101.5 x 127 cm
Inv. No. 6764

Acquired on the art market in 1928, the present painting combines all the characteristics typical of Cavallino's early period: almost alone among the Neapolitan painters of his generation, he endowed his compositions with tender, poetic features. Elegant postures as well as sensitive action and reaction dominate the artistically arranged scene. This prevailing mood is rendered mysterious with the distinctive use of chiaroscuro: Cavallino places one of the three kings at the centre of the painting, thus providing a strong, brightly lit foreground figure *(repoussoir)* to create greater depth. The imposingly sweeping movement of his precious cloak is set off against powerful shadows and finds its formal counterpart in the gold chain in the background, while other large areas of the painting are punctuated by back lighting. Naturalistic elements, such as the fur hat of the man at the left edge of the painting and the sensitive depiction of the surface of the royal garment, are evidence of Cavallino's training under the Spaniard José de Ribera (1591–1652), who worked in Naples. The complexity of the composition is created by the crossing of compositional lines and the spatial refinement, which are actually older, Mannerist principles for which the painter took his inspiration from the graphic works of Bartholomäus Spranger (Cat. No. 55) and Hendrick Goltzius.

WOLFGANG HEIMBACH
(Ovelgönne near Oldenburg,
ca. 1613 – Ovelgönne near
Oldenburg, after 1678?)
1640
Copper, 62 x 114 cm
Inv. No. 599

Wolfgang Heimbach ranked among the few important northern German painters of the 17th century. Born a deaf mute, he probably found a noble patron in Count Anton Günther von Oldenburg, who financed the painter's journey to the Netherlands in the 1630s. This trip would shape his future style: under the influence of the Caravaggio followers of the Utrecht school (Baburen, Terbrugghen, Honthorst) and genre-painters such as Dirck Hals, he specialised in nocturnal, mostly candle-lit genre scenes. Around 1637 Heimbach embarked on a journey to Italy and made a stopover in Vienna (on his return trip?), where he painted the present *Banquet at Night* and probably also a portrait of Archduke Leopold Wilhelm (KHM, GG, Inv. No. 9820).

The atmosphere of the scene illuminated by strong candle-light is created by the magnificent juxtaposition of brightly lit and *contre-jour* (back-lit) elements. The tiled stove on the left, the Brussels tapestries on the walls and the wooden coffered ceiling provide the setting for the banquet. We know the identity of the impressive room: the seemingly noble group has gathered in the Knights' Hall of Vienna's Hofburg. Heimbach consistently keeps to a horizontal structure, creating depth of perspective only through expressive lighting effects. This compositional severity is effectively countered by individual figures in the foreground and – upon closer examination – the apparently relaxed mood of the participants, free from courtly etiquette.

78 ALLEGORY OF VANITY (VANITAS)

LEONAERT BRAMER
(Delft, 1596 – Delft, 1674)
Ca. 1640/45
Wood, 80 x 61.3 cm
Inv. No. 413

In the present depiction of Vanity, as well as in its companion piece (*Allegory of Vanity;* KHM, GG, Inv. No. 417), Bramer presents a wide spectrum of allegorical objects and figures, which keep alive the memory of the transience of all earthly things. Wrapped in a fur cape and adorned with gold jewellery, a woman sitting in a penumbra contemplates her aged face in a mirror. Other luxury articles are spread out carelessly on the table in front of her, while parts of a magnificent suit of armour are scattered on the floor. The picture is enclosed on the right by a number of damaged musical instruments, some propped against the table, some lying on the floor. A lute-player, dressed in black and illuminated by a bright beam of light, marks the top of the triangular composition.

In a manner comparable to the slumped figure of the musician, the wood of the instruments appears to have lost its solidity. Beauty, fortune, wartime fame and the sound of an instrument: all of these are ultimately transient and will fall into decay. The painterly realisation is in line with this subject: a musty basic colour prevails. In the 16th and 17th centuries such allegories of Vanity, mostly realised as still-life or genre paintings, were found mainly in the northern Netherlands and Germany.

JACOB JORDAENS
(Antwerp, 1593 –
Antwerp, 1678)
Ca. 1640/45
Canvas, 242 x 300 cm
Inv. No. 786

Jordaens's energetic compositions would be inconceivable without the paintings of Rubens to which the younger artist sometimes contributed. But he combined the influence of his mentor with a selection of burlesque, coarse and common physiognomies (showing the influence of the Netherlands successors to Caravaggio in both this and the usually close-up view) to create his own, unmistakeable style. In presenting "laughing but didactic" contents, Jordaens is also assimilating modern Dutch influences: in the Protestant Netherlands moralising genre paintings – always, however, in small format – were much more highly esteemed than in Catholic Flanders.

Raised above their everyday cares and united in song, costumes, drunkenness and gluttony, the revellers are pressed into the smallest conceivable space. Several days earlier, at Epiphany (Twelfth Night), they had bought slips of paper with the names of various court offices, and to choose the "king" a cake had been made containing a single bean. The guest who found the bean in his piece became the king of the feast. But Jordaens does not leave the choice of the protagonist to chance: the oldest participant is wearing the crown, and he has chosen the prettiest woman as his "queen". This touches on a theme that had been widespread since the 16th century but was usually depicted in isolation: the "odd couple". Now the rest of the citizens are being assigned their respective roles. On the right, above the king's massive head, the "royal taster" is performing his duties. The "doctor" in the left foreground is relieving himself in dangerous proximity to the food. In the foreground is the poorly illuminated but powerful figure of the "equerry", who has already lost his slip of paper. His body has an important function in the composition: it stabilises and provides rhythm to the other figures in the painting, who are depicted with slight foreshortening. Discreetly in the background is an inscription on a cartouche: "nil similus insano quam ebrius" – "nothing is more like a madman than a drunk".

BERNARDO STROZZI
(Genoa, 1581 –
Venice, 1644)
Ca. 1643/44
Canvas, 135 x 120 cm
Inv. No. 256

Bernardo Strozzi received the epithet of "Il prete Genovese" ("the Genoese priest") when he fled to Venice in 1630. A member of the Capuchin monastery in Genoa, he had managed to be granted the privilege of leading a secular life in 1610. Now he sought to escape his duties as a clergyman for good. He succeeded because he was under papal protection and the more liberal city of Venice thus did not prosecute him. While still in Genoa, Strozzi had studied the works of the Genoa-based painters Simon Vouet and Orazio Gentileschi, who were influenced by Caravaggio. In Venice, at the beginning of his late period, Strozzi was increasingly influenced by the works of Rubens, van Dyck and Veronese. This was an eclectic process, but he nonetheless succeeded in developing his own style, which is characterised by rich and bright colours, dearly visible brush strokes, dramatic use of light and a specific emphasis on the body language of his characters.

John the Baptist explains his mission to the priests and Levites sent from Jerusalem (John 1:19–28), who eagerly ask him about his task. St. John is seen standing in front of a small group of listeners. He is characterised by the camel skin draped over his slender body and the band in his left hand, marking with the word "ecce" the beginning of the traditional reference to the Lamb of God ("Behold the Lamb of God, which taketh away the sin of the world", John 1:29). With his carefully chosen, close-up compositional detail, Strozzi reveals only part of the scene to the viewer. None of the figures depicted in front of a landscape is fully visible. With the help of the "empty" centre, the beholder's attention is fully drawn to the gestures and facial expressions of the participants in the scene. The clear differences in age allude to the fact that John the Baptist's mission is directed at everyone and thus universally applicable.

81 ARCHDUKE LEOPOLD WILLIAM IN HIS GALLERY AT BRUSSELS

DAVID TENIERS THE
YOUNGER
(Antwerp, 1610 –
Brussels, 1690)
Ca. 1651
Canvas, 123 x 163 cm
Inv. No. 739

In the first half of the 17th century, the affluent citizens of Brussels and Antwerp became interested in establishing their own private galleries. They were inspired in this desire by a celebrated model, one, however, that they could never hope to match: the collection begun in the early 17th century by the Spanish regent in Brussels. Parallel to this, and only in the southern Netherlands, a type of painting developed in which picture galleries were shown.

During his regency (1647–1656), the most important Habsburg collector, Archduke Leopold Wilhelm, assembled some 1400 paintings. This view of his gallery is likely fictitious in part because the high room with windows on the left is probably not exactly like any space that existed at the time. The size and proportions of some of the decoratively hung pictures have been altered, in reality, they could never have been hung in that combination. Here David Teniers, chamberlain, court painter and keeper of the archduke's art collection, is accompanying the scholarly collector on a visit to his gallery. On the left, other visitors are grouped around a table, among them the diminutive castle chaplain, painter and later gallery director Antonius van der Baren. Among the elements often found in views of picture galleries are the paintings propped up in the foreground and the opening of the perspective to the rear, sometimes through a door or, as here, through large windows.

Early examples of this type sometimes feature Christian didactic content, conveyed by a selection of pictures depicted in miniature; the portraits of Leopold Wilhelm's gallery (nine in all), however, serve a purely ostentatious purpose. The one now in Vienna was sent to Prague by the brother of its owner, Emperor Ferdinand III, as evidence of the wealth of the archduke's picture gallery. Most of the 51 Italian works shown in this painting are today in the Kunsthistorisches Museum.

REMBRANDT
HARMENSZOON VAN RIJN
(Leiden, 1606 –
Amsterdam, 1669)
1652
Canvas, 112 x 81.5 cm
Inv. No. 411

There is much evidence that Rembrandt's series of almost forty reliably documented self-portraits – unique in the history of painting – served as more than merely a vehicle for the Amsterdam painter's self-reflection. They were also a suitable means for him to present himself to the public: a form of self-marketing.

The term "self-portrait" was not yet common in 17th-century Holland; such a painting was more likely to be referred to as "a portrait of Rembrandt painted by himself". Thus for the ambitious collector, the painting was two things: Rembrandt's image and at the same time an example of his art.

Rembrandt has concentrated the meagre light on his face. His simple garment, trimmed only at the shoulders and collar, is gently illuminated and only hints at his stature. Entirely fixated on the ageing facial features, the viewer is initially distracted from the self-confident, almost challenging posture. The two thumbs hooked into a belt that seems to have been cursorily tied at the waist are a self-confident antipode to the melancholy, complexly painted countenance. Rembrandt's face is further emphasised by its contrast to other parts of the portrait with their uniformly thick application of paint, in general a characteristic of his late works. In contrast to earlier self-portraits in which the artist is often dressed in sumptuous fabrics, Rembrandt has chosen a simple garment; perhaps it is even the artist's smock that he actually wore in his studio.

83 THE GREAT FOREST

JACOB VAN RUISDAEL
(Haarlern, ca. 1628/29 –
Amsterdam?, 1682)
Ca. 1655/60
Canvas, 139 x 180 cm
Inv. No. 426

There is a long tradition in Netherlandish landscape painting of depicting forests. The first purely forest landscape was created by the southern German painter Albrecht Altdorfer (*St. George in the Forest*, 1510; Munich, Alte Pinakothek). In the mid-15th century the theme can be found in the graphic works of Pieter Bruegel the Elder, and it is also seen before 1600 in the paintings of the Flemish artist Gillis van Coninxloo (1544–1606), who had immigrated to the Northern Netherlands. Initially the depiction of the sky was not important in these compositions. Only in paintings after 1600 does the viewer see the image from a greater distance, peering into the dark isolation of a forest, while the horizon expands and the sky contributes significantly to the atmosphere of the scene. Unlike their Flemish counterparts (cf. Cat. No. 66), Northern Netherlandish landscape painters mostly refrained from adding Christian or mythological human or animal figures as accessories (staffage). Jacob van Ruisdael, whose œuvre includes more than 700 paintings, ranks among the most important Dutch landscape painters of the second half of the 17th century. He was reasonably paid for his works, although the painters of "Italian" landscapes received larger sums.

The composition of this large-format painting is extremely well-balanced: the dimensions of the foreground, a prelude to the main theme, allow the viewer to keep a necessary distance without losing sight of the heroic vastness of the forest (and thus of nature). A path crossed by a stream provides structure, creating a diagonal effect of depth. The tiny figures of the traveller taking a rest and the couple approaching the ford provide the necessary sense of scale.

REMBRANDT
HARMENSZOON VAN RIJN
(Leiden, 1606 –
Amsterdam, 1669)
Ca. 1656/57
Canvas, 70.5 x 64 cm
Inv. No. 410

Titus was born in 1641, the fourth child of the painter and his first wife, Saskia, and the only one to reach adulthood. After 1659, he and his father's mistress, Hendrickje Stoffels, ran Rembrandt's business, the father having lost his fortune because of his lavish lifestyle and a bad investment about which the archives do not provide adequate information. A court had previously found the artist to be legally incompetent. The son died, however, in 1668, a year before his father.

Titus is seated in an armchair, intently reading a book he holds in his hands. His mouth is slightly open, suggesting great focus of attention and giving the scene a subtle immediacy. He appears relaxed, his full attention turned away from the viewer. The light is concentrated on his forehead, hands and book, further strengthening the intimate immediacy of the moment. Rembrandt often used his son as a model. Although Titus has no particular "role" to play here, there is a strong focus on the act of reading, and this takes precedence over the son's physiognomy.

DIEGO RODRÍGUEZ DE
SILVA Y VELÁZQUEZ
(Seville, 1599 –
Madrid, 1660)
1659
Canvas, 127 x 107 cm
Inv. No. 2130

In his second marriage, King Philip IV of Spain, the father of Margarita Teresa (1651–1673), was married to his niece Maria Anna, a daughter of Emperor Ferdinand III. Margarita became engaged to her uncle, the later Emperor Leopold I, at an early age (they wed in 1666). She died in Vienna in 1673, during her seventh pregnancy. The imposing portrait shows the infanta at the age of eight and was sent to the Vienna court as a gift the same year it was painted.

For forty years, Velázquez succeeded in defending his leading position at the Spanish court against ambitious rivals. Unlike Rubens, for example, who from the very beginning had secured himself a great degree of independence while in the employ of the Spanish regents in Brussels, Velázquez remained obligated to fulfil the classical duties of a court painter. In the portraits regularly commissioned by members of the royal family, he maintained the traditional gestures and accessories of the court portrait but revolutionised their painterly realisation: the stature of the splendidly dressed child gains unity and three-dimensional quality only from a certain distance. The cool, metallic effect of her garment provides a contrast to the delicate skin and is reflected in her blue eyes. In this late work Velázquez achieved a perfect balance between the duty to paint an official portrait and a desire to depict the individual in a lifelike manner.

In the 18th century the picture – which was already a fragment of the original – was cut down again to an oval shape. It was restored to its (approximately) original form in 1923.

86 THE DEATH OF CLEOPATRA

GUIDO CAGNACCI,
CALLED GUIDO CANLASSI
(Sant'Arcangelo di Romagna,
1601 – Vienna, 1663)
1659/63
Canvas, 140 x 159.5 cm
Inv. No. 260

Beginning in the Renaissance period, the world of literature and art rejected the Christian perception of suicide as being a reprehensible act and oriented itself on those trends of classical philosophy that celebrated suicide, in certain cases, as a logical and courageous act. Starting in the 16th century, heroines became a popular subject of paintings and were sometimes joined together in a series of so-called *donne famose* (famous, heroic women).

Guido Cagnacci received his training in Bologna and Rome and had lived in Rimini since the beginning of the 1620s. As early as 1648 he was running his own workshop in Venice. He accepted an appointment as court painter to Emperor Leopold I in 1660 and spent the last years of his life in Vienna.

In this painting of Cleopatra, the last of this subject in his œuvre, he combines two conflicting artistic trends: the realistic and expressive gestures and facial expressions of the servants, some in touching grief, some in agitated observation, have been influenced by Caravaggio's successors and juxtaposed to the classical posture of the dying Cleopatra, adopted from Guido Reni and Correggio. Equally charged with tension is the contrast between the monochromatic background and the open display of the gently lit female nudes. The deadly bite of the uraeus serpent, coiled tenderly around Cleopatra's arm, is the focus of the servants' attention; the view of the beholder, however, is mainly directed to the sensuality of Cleopatra's body, set against the deep red fabric of her throne.

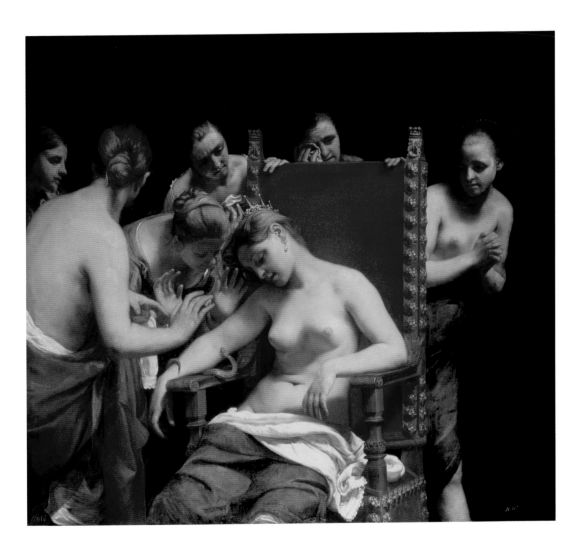

FRANS VAN MIERIS
THE ELDER
(Leiden, 1635 –
Leiden, 1681)
1660
Wood, 54.2 x 42.7 cm
Inv. No. 586

Frans van Mieris and his teacher Gerrit Dou were the most prominent proponents of the so-called "fine paintings" created in Leiden. The characteristic features of these genre scenes were their small format, great detail and the fact that they were sometimes painted on gilt copper. Mieris's works were sold during his lifetime at remarkably high prices that made them less than easily affordable, even for such wealthy buyers as Archduke Leopold Wilhelm.

The painter has used powerful illumination to create an interior that is readily comprehensible to the viewer. Every surface is depicted with great care and sensitivity, and the brushstrokes are no longer visible. The viewer is witness to a sales talk that, at the same time, is also an erotic encounter between a man and a woman. An apparently affluent customer is assessing the quality of the fabric laid out before him (in the background on the left are the other goods, stacked neatly on shelves). At the same time he touches the delicate chin of his interlocutor, gazing at her approvingly. This comparison is certainly intended to be ambiguous. Mieris has provided a hidden written message: in the folds of the carpet on the table in the right foreground is a silver band with the word "comparare", which has several meanings in Latin, including "to buy" and "to compare". It remains open which of the goods will find a buyer here: the precious fabric or the woman's love. An old man crouches beneath the fireplace mantle along the back wall. Perhaps his concerned facial expression is intended to be the painter's admonishing reference to the kind of business that is about to be concluded: but does the old man view the proceedings as immoral or is he perhaps a procurer?

JAN STEEN
(Leiden, 1626/36? –
Leiden, 1679)
1663
Canvas, 105 x 145 cm
Inv. No. 791

Jan Steen arranges the various actors as though on a theatre stage. The gentle depth of the composition is based on a triangle, with the magnificently dressed young woman at its top point. Her clothing and seductive look identify her as a "loose-living" girl. She, however, is not the focus of the scene; that is provided by the lady of the house, who has fallen asleep at the table on the left. Her "absence" has resulted in the rest of the story: the dog is finishing the meat pie that was served on the table, one of the children is filching something from the cabinet on the wall ("opportunity makes the thief"), the little girl's brother is trying out a pipe, and the youngest child, sitting in his highchair, is playing carelessly with a string of pearls. His attention diverted to the side, a young man is trying to play a violin. Young people who continued to live at home were considered suspect in the popular culture of the Netherlands at the time. The prostitute in the foreground has already been mentioned: in a provocative gesture she holds a filled glass between the legs of the man of the house, while he dismisses with a grin the admonishment of the nun (a Beguine?) standing on the right. The duck on the shoulder of the man next to her identifies him as a Quaker, who urges the reading of pious texts. Finally, the pig in the doorway to the kitchen is an allusion to another proverb: "Neither cast ye your pearls [here: roses] before swine". Hanging above the heads of these sinners are the symbols of the penalty to be expected for unbridled, lustful behaviour: a sword and a crutch in a basket suspended from the ceiling.

The painting's traditional German title *"Die verkehrte Welt"* ("The Topsy-Turvy World") is not completely in accordance with the content, because this is really a humorous warning against one of the seven deadly sins, *luxuria* (extravagance, later lust). An interesting biographic detail: at times Steen had to earn a living by running an inn and a brewery.

89 WOMAN AND CHILD WITH SERVING MAID

PIETER DE HOOCH
(Rotterdam, 1629 –
Amsterdam, 1684)
Ca. 1663/65
Canvas, 64 x 76 cm
Inv. No. 5976

The paintings by this artist, who worked in both Delft and Amsterdam, repeatedly demonstrate his interest in depicting exactly defined spaces. De Hooch was part of an artistic movement that was later called the Delft school: another member was Johannes Vermeer (Cat. No. 90), three years younger than de Hooch and more prominent today. This type of usually small-format painting of an interior became a fixed part of the local artistic repertoire. There is also a characteristic manner of dealing with light: both de Hooch and Vermeer used soft illumination, bathing their paintings in a gentle, flattering light. De Hooch painted the present work during his time in Amsterdam (starting in 1660), where he specialised in depicting the style of home furnishings and life typical of the city's well-situated citizens.

Despite the presence of a serving maid, the elegantly clad mother is caring personally for her infant; she does not waste money on a wet-nurse. Across the spotless tile floor, we look into a second room at the back, then through the half-open door to a house on a canal and the city beyond. A fire is burning on the hearth, providing a colourful accent that recurs in the infant's clothing and the sunlit view. In a similarly rhythmic fashion, the red of the fabric drying on the hearth is repeated at several points in the picture, giving the composition a balance of colour.

This scene makes clear the understanding of (ideal) roles at the time: attentive childcare and a well-run household are a woman's province. Thus the opening to the city, which makes sense from a compositional point of view, also has symbolic character: the outside world is a man's domain, but the female sphere always remains open to him.

JOHANNES VERMEER
VAN DELFT
(Delft, 1632 – Delft, 1675)
Ca. 1666/68
Canvas, 120 x 100 cm
Inv. No. 9128

The painter himself probably gave this large-format interior its title. In 1663 and 1670 Vermeer was chairman of the Artists' Guild of St. Luke, but if the painting was intended as programmatic gift to the guild as an allegorical depiction of the arts and trades represented in that organisation, it was never presented to its intended owners: *The Art of Painting* is mentioned in the inventory of Vermeer's estate. It is highly likely that he used the painting to demonstrate his mastery of this art.

The drawn-back curtain opens a view of a room that is bathed in light from a window on the left (not visible in the picture). On the back wall is a detailed map of the Netherlands. In the foreground a chair and the table behind it, covered with various articles, direct the viewer's gaze to the middle distance. His back towards the viewer, the painter sits at his easel; he has begun work on a half-length portrait of the girl standing at the window. Thus painting occupies the most prominent place among the arts. The articles on the table represent sculpture (plaster cast), art printing (book) and tapestry weaving (fabrics). But what is the meaning of the model the artist is painting? The female figure is holding a trumpet and a book in her hands and is wearing a laurel wreath in her hair. Thus she is Clio, the Muse of history. Classical art theory considered history to be the primary subject of painting, but Vermeer subtly resists this doctrine, which in any case was almost irrelevant in the Dutch art market. With great painterly assertion, he raises this "inferior" interior to the ranks of highest art and lends this view of a painter's work the qualities of an allegory. With his perfect balance of pictorial elements, poetic tranquillity and great sensuality of colour, the artist creates an atmosphere of enormous elegance and harmony. In order to accurately depict interior spaces, Vermeer used various technical aids, which probably included the forerunner of the modern camera, the camera obscura.

LUCA GIORDANO
(Naples, 1634 –
Naples, 1705)
Ca. 1666
Canvas, 419 x 283 cm
Inv. No. 350

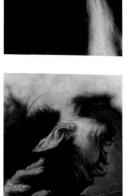

An unusually large body of work, an apparently easily achieved virtuosity of composition as well as stylistic and technical diversity and improvisation: these are the trademarks of this artist, who worked mainly in Naples but later (1692–1702) also at the royal court of Spain. At the same time, his paintings display – and this applies particularly to the one in Vienna – the dominating influence of the works of José de Ribera. Their appearance is characterised by the use of chiaroscuro, a drastic narrative style and an application of colour that is in part naturalistic (e.g. inspired by the surfaces that are depicted). In addition, Giordano increasingly used Venetian coloration after his stay in the city on the lagoon in 1665. His "style" also changed within a single picture depending on the criteria of content. In the present painting Giordano has used great richness of invention to present the anguished downfall of those who have fallen from grace. The red of the fires of Hell is reflected on their bodies, which are depicted with a restless brush in pastose paint. Giordano depicts the archangel, however, in thin, flowing paint as a Classical-Roman figure. Michael is an effortless victor, fighting gracefully and elegantly.

It is not known who originally commissioned the altarpiece, which came to Vienna at an early date. The barons Bartolotti von Partenfeld renovated the chapel of St. Louis in Vienna's Minorite Church in the late 17th century, and in 1698 donated Giordano's work for the new altar.

FRANCESCO SOLIMENA
(Canale di Serino, 1657 –
Barra near Naples, 1747)
1728
Canvas, 309 x 284 cm
Inv. No. 1601

In early 1728, Francesco Solimena, who dominated Neapolitan painting in the first half of the 18th century and was successful at other courts as well, was commissioned to create this painting. Influenced by Luca Giordano (Cat. No. 91) in his early works, Solimena ultimately developed a highly individual style, characterised by dramatic and rapid changes of light and colour.

Gundacker Ludwig, Count Althann had been Director of Imperial Buildings since 1716 and was involved with Fischer von Erlach in the projects to expand Vienna's Hofburg Palace. In 1726 he was appointed Chief Inspector of the Imperial Academy of Painting and Sculpture. During his administration, a three-volume inventory with 120 copperplate engravings was drawn up of the Imperial Painting Gallery in Vienna's Stallburg (Anton J. von Prenner, *Theatrum artis pictoriae: in quo Tabulae depictae quae in Caesarea Vindobonensi Pinacotheca servantur leviore caelatura aeri insculptae exhibentur*, Viennae Austriae 1728). Fama, the personification of earthly fame, accompanies the solemn presentation of the inventory to Charles VI in this perfect example of a late Baroque tribute to a ruler. However, the form in which Solimena originally delivered the large-format work in April 1728 was apparently not completely in keeping with the court's ideal of ostentation. In Vienna, Johann Gottfried Auerbach replaced the faces of the protagonists, who had originally been turned towards one another with emotion, with the portraits seen here, which gaze stiffly from the picture, thus creating distance to the scene and to reality.

93 THE DEPOSITION

FRANCESCO SOLIMENA
(Canale di Serino, 1657 –
Barra near Naples, 1747)
Ca. 1731
Canvas, 398 x 223 cm
Inv. No. 3507

After the Kingdom of Naples-Sicily came under Habsburg rule as a result of treaties ending the War of the Spanish Succession (1713 and 1714), it seemed an obvious choice to hire one of the most successful painters in Naples, Francesco Solimena, for projects in the imperial capital of Vienna and the surrounding area. Prince Eugene of Savoy had been commander in chief during the wars against the Turks and the War of the Spanish Succession and was also one of the most important architectural patrons of Baroque Vienna. He commissioned Solimena to create an altarpiece for Schlosshof, the hunting lodge that he had remodelled to the east of the capital in 1726.

Here the artist created a lively interplay of light and shadow but did so in a manner that was different from Caravaggio's (Cat. Nos. 58, 59). Solimena's chiaroscuro serves not to clarify the composition but rather to separate the bodies into their individual component parts, creating a fragmented surface that makes a restless impression. The ladders and the Cross, which Nicodemus has climbed up to from behind, counter this fragmentation by creating a strong formal framework. Christ's body is being handed down from above and is already in steady hands below. The viewer's gaze is led first to the body and then directed by the extended right arm of the crimson-clad Joseph of Arimathea to the group of mourning women. A deathly pale Virgin Mary makes their importance clear and contributes to the stability and legibility of the composition. The mirror-image facial expressions of Christ and Mary have a highly emotional quality, and there is a correspondingly nervous use of colour. These principles were later developed further by Rococo painters, especially in Central Europe. Francesco Solimena was their most important predecessor and forerunner.

THOMAS GAINSBOROUGH
(Sudbury, 1727 –
London, 1788)
Ca.1748
Canvas, 66 x 95 cm
Inv. No. 6271

It is remarkable that Gainsborough, who lived in an age when the "grand tour" became an essential element in the life of England's aristocracy and affluent middle classes, never left his native land. He apparently found sufficient opportunity to study important examples of Dutch landscape painting in high-quality English collections. The son of John Gainsborough, a maker of woollen goods, he opened his own studio in London in 1744 after several years of training but moved to Ipswich two years later. There he received his first portrait commissions from members of the English aristocracy. (Decades later, in 1780, Gainsborough became the official portraitist of the royal family.) In Ipswich he also painted a series of landscape paintings, among them the present work, which was acquired for the imperial collection in 1913.

The shallow pond on the left surrounded by gnarled trees and the view of the winding path leading into the distance are traditional motifs of Dutch painting. Only a small patch of the horizon is visible, and it is further constricted by a country house placed at its centre. The dark clouds that tower above the scenery correspond in their form and colour to the basic shades of the landscape lying below them; the small body of water reflects the blue of the sky. Only the luminescent red clothing of the staffage figure resting at the side of the path disturbs the unified scheme of coloration. Remarkable is the Rococo-style lightness and agility with which the paint has been applied. In contrast to Ruisdael's heavy, "heroic" landscape (cf. Cat. No. 83), this one is "elegant and casual", and thus more in keeping with the character of the English aristocracy.

95   VIENNA VIEWED FROM THE BELVEDERE PALACE

BERNARDO BELLOTTO,
CALLED CANALETTO
(Venice, 1722 –
Warsaw, 1780)
1759/60
Canvas, 135 x 213 cm
Inv. No. 1669

The view from the Upper Belvedere Palace across a Vienna that had flourished and expanded following the second Turkish siege in 1683 is probably the most well-known of the views commissioned by Empress Maria Theresa. These depict palaces (Schönbrunn and Schlosshof) as well as urban scenes (Cat. No. 96).

Bellotto's stay in Vienna is framed by his departure from Dresden in December 1758 and his arrival in Munich in January 1761. No documents concerning the empress's commission have been preserved. It is also impossible to reconstruct with certainty the programme that determined the choice of subjects or the place the paintings were originally intended to decorate, but perhaps it was Pressburg (now the capital of Slovakia, Bratislava). Today all thirteen paintings in the series are in the Kunsthistorisches Museum.

There is no proof that Bellotto used a camera obscura but it may be assumed that he did so. The device was universally recognised as an aid to drawing in the Netherlandish and German painting of the 16th century. From there it travelled to Italy, where Bellotto's uncle and teacher, Antonio Canal, used it in making his numerous views of Venice. Both painters, however, altered the images they made with this technical assistance, changing them to create compositions that were more artistically satisfying and took the perception of the human eye into account. In the present view, the placement of the vertical elements – the Church of St. Charles Borromeo (Karlskirche) on the left, the tower of St. Stephen's Cathedral in the middle, and the dome of the Salesian Church on the right – differs from the actual situation in that here they are an equal distance apart and closer together. Still surrounded by defensive fortifications, the city centre appears unified and relatively distant, extending towards the foot-hills of the Vienna Woods. The sharply delineated shadows are given particular importance in the composition; in the strictly structured gardens that extend from the ground floor of the palace, they provide rhythm and strengthen the impression of depth in the composition. Enlivening the scene is the addition of numerous small accessory figures (staffage); they make clear the sharply foreshortened (but in reality considerable) length of the pathway between the Upper and Lower Belvedere Palaces.

BERNARDO BELLOTTO,
CALLED CANALETTO
(Venice, 1722 –
Warsaw, 1780)
1759/60
Canvas, 115 x 155.5 cm
Inv. No. 1672

In 1851 the street level of Postgasse in Vienna's first district was lowered by several metres. In order to assure access to the portal of the Dominican Church, which had been completed in 1675, a double set of outdoor stairs was built. Bellotto's view depicts the original situation, with the long façade of the Jesuit Seminary, on which construction began in 1623, occupying the right half of the painting. At the end of the street is the Jesuit Observatory in its original state; the upper floors of the building were later removed. The existing architecture initially created a problem for the painter: on the left side is the Baroque church façade with a structure of sculptural elements, while across from it is the horizontal, flat façade of the seminary with its regular pattern of windows. It is difficult to create a convincing perspective out of such irregularly distributed visual elements. As so often before and later, Bellotto solved this problem by using distinct shadows and by combining the various standpoints. In contrast to the sharp contours of the masonry, the staffage figures, coach, crates and barrels of the stalls seem soft and pastose. They enliven the monumental architectural setting, making it seem untouched by (human) transience.

For the painting's background history cf. Cat. No. 95.

97 EMPEROR JOSEPH II WITH GRAND DUKE PIETRO LEOPOLDO OF TUSCANY

POMPEO BATONI
(Lucca, 1708 – Rome, 1787)
1769
Canvas, 173 x 122 cm
Inv. No. 1628

Joseph II (1741–1790, emperor from 1765) arrived in Rome on 15 March 1769. Together with his younger brother Pietro Leopoldo (1747–1792, grand duke of Tuscany from 1765, emperor as Leopold II from 1790) he visited the city's sights during his two-week stay and was a guest at many official receptions – a schedule that was typical of a grand tour.

Pompeo Batoni had an extremely high reputation as a portraitist among aristocratic visitors to Rome. He and Anton Raphael Mengs were the most prominent Roman proponents of a new, Classicistic approach to portraiture. Among the celebrated qualities of his painting were the fine and precise delineation he had learned while training as a goldsmith and his "ornamental elegance". Joseph II and Pietro Leopoldo visited Batoni's studio in via Bocca di Leone six times for morning sittings. In June of 1769, the finished and already much-admired work was presented to Pope Clement XIV before making its way to the Vienna court.

The brothers are depicted in rather simple dress and a relaxed posture, their amicable relationship expressed by the gentle gesture of their clasped hands. The restrained character of the portrait is in keeping with the self-image of an enlightened monarch. One of the most important works of the French Enlightenment, Montesquieu's *De l'esprit des loix* (English edition: *The Spirit of Laws,* 1750), is lying alongside a city map of Rome on the small table at the right. Pietro Leopoldo stands at the left, wearing the Order of the Golden Fleece, while his brother the emperor is wearing the star and cross of the Military Order of Maria Theresa and of the Royal Hungarian Order of St. Stephen. Given the history of its creation, this portrait with its Roman ambience has also preserved the two subjects for posterity as educated travellers to Italy.

ANTON RAPHAEL MENGS
(Aussig, Bohemia [now Ústí
nad Labem, Czech Republic],
1728 – Rome, 1779)
Ca. 1773/74
Wood, 114 x 86 cm
Inv. No. 124

In the Gospel of Matthew, the apostle relates: "And when [the wise men] were departed, behold, the angel of the Lord appeareth to Joseph in a dream, saying, Arise, and take the young child and his mother, and flee into Egypt, and be thou there until I bring thee word: for Herod will seek the young child to destroy him." (Matt. 2:13.)

In 1773 Mengs was granted the privilege of hanging his portrait in the Florence gallery of artists' portraits founded by Giorgio Vasari in the mid-16th century. Allegedly, he chose the spot himself: having been celebrated as "the new Raphael", he promptly placed his portrait beneath the one of the great Italian painter. In 1745 Mengs had become Saxon court painter in Dresden but spent a great deal of his time in Rome. There, along with Winckelmann, he became one of the founders of Classicism and in the view of his admirers helped to supersede the decadent Baroque. In 1773/74 he returned to Madrid, where he had been appointed court painter to Charles III in 1760.

The present painting depicting Joseph's dream was probably created during Mengs's Florentine period and came directly into the possession of the grand duke Pietro Leopoldo. In Rome Mengs had renewed his study of the works of Michelangelo, and Joseph's posture is clearly adopted from the master's *Jerome* in the Sistine Chapel.

JOSEPH SIFFRED DUPLESSIS
(Carpentras, 1725 –
Versailles, 1802)
1775
Canvas, 99.5 x 80.5 cm
Inv. No. 1795

In the spring and summer of 1774, Christoph Willibald Gluck (Erasbach near Neumarkt, Upper Palatinate, 1714 – Vienna, 1787) had scored triumphal success in Paris with two operas in his new style, *Iphigénie en Aulide* and *Orphée et Euridice*. At the same time, Joseph Siffred Duplessis was working on a portrait of the French king Louis XVI. The painter was later granted the privilege of living in the Louvre. His rise to success was meteoric: only in 1769 had Parisian critics finally accepted the artist into the community of recognised portraitists. At that time the acknowledged authority and publisher of the pioneering work *Encyclopédie ou Dictionnaire raisonné des sciences, des arts et des métiers,* Denis Diderot, expressed his astonishment that it had taken so long for the quality of Duplessis' works to be recognised.

In 1774 Gluck was the sensation of the Paris Salon, and the artist seized the opportunity of painting a portrait of the prominent guest from Vienna. The composer is seated, his upper body and face turned towards the viewer, at a spinet indicated in the foreground. But he is not looking at either the keys or the music, and his left hand hovers above the instrument. Gluck's eyes are directed over the head of the viewer. In this, Duplessis is adopting a Christian pictorial tradition that is found in early medieval depictions of divine inspiration. This look in which the subject pauses for a moment of concentration, turning the eyes upwards, is later also found in the iconography of St. Cecilia, the patron saint of music. Taken in by this depiction of the creative act, the viewer overlooks the fact that little is attractive about the composer's scarred face. All of this makes the painting a unique musician's portrait focused on the most important point, the act of composing.

J. S. Duplessis
pinx. parisis 1775

FRANCESCO GUARDI
(Venice, 1712 –
Venice, 1793)
After 1776
Canvas, 29 x 45 cm
Inv. No. 6234

With free and easy pastose brushstrokes and light colours, Guardi painted a variation on a composition created in the 1730s by his great Venetian predecessor Antonio Canal, called Canaletto (1697–1768). In Venice, Canaletto had developed the *veduta* (Italian: "view") into a special form of landscape painting and found a wide clientele of patrons and purchasers, especially among affluent English tourists. In the work of Canaletto's nephew, Bernardo Bellotto (Cat. Nos. 95, 96), the architectural *veduta* became a European phenomenon; Guardi continued to develop the type, but only in Venice. In contrast to Canaletto and Bellotto, he was less exact in the depiction of his scenes: in his paintings the city of Venice seems highly idealised and flooded with magical light. The architecture and the figures added as accessories (staffage) combine to create a unified atmosphere.

Guardi chose a motif for the present painting that was not among the main attractions for 18th-century travellers. Instead he represented Venetian military power, which was no longer in its heyday. In 1570, before the great sea battle between the Christian and Turkish forces at Lepanto, the Venetian Arsenal had produced about a hundred warships in only a short time. The extensive shipyard stretches out behind the impressive gate at the centre of the composition. This small-format *veduta* was acquired for the imperial collection in 1912, along with its counterpart (*St. Mark's Square in Venice;* KHM, GG, Inv. No. 6233).

APPENDIX

GLOSSARY

ALLEGORY: (from Greek: *allegorein,* to speak figuratively). The concrete representation in painting, sculpture and poetry of abstract concepts, ideas and intellectual relationships. In contrast to the symbol – although the boundary has not always been strictly drawn – allegory is usually expressed by personification, using a human (less frequently an animal) figure: e.g., Amor to represent love, a lovely girl as youth, a skeleton with a scythe as death, etc.

CAMERA OBSCURA: (from Latin: "dark chamber"). A small darkened room or box admitting its only light through a tiny hole. A reverse, upside-down image is cast on the wall opposite the hole and can be viewed or drawn. The principle was familiar to Aristotle (384 – 322 BC), and starting in the 16th century it was used by painters and scientists to create true-to-life drawings. It was an ancestor of the photographic camera (invented in 1826).

CARAVAGGIST: There is no evidence that Caravaggio had either pupils or assistants, but his works were widely imitated internationally in the first decades after his death. Groups of painters in Italy, the Netherlands and France were strongly influenced by Caravaggio's chiaroscuro effects and his specific realism. Hendrick Terbrugghen, Gerrit van Honthorst (who spent many years in Rome) and Dirck van Baburen made Utrecht a centre of Caravaggism.

COLORATION: choice and arrangement of colours, colour effect. The overall effect of a picture results from the selection of colours and the differentiation of colour values.

DIPTYCH: (from Greek: *diptychos,* folded in two). In antiquity the name referred to a hinged writing tablet of two wooden, metal or ivory panels in upright format fastened together with string or straps. The inner side of the panels was coated with wax, and a stylus could be used for writing on the waxed surface. By peeling and smoothing the surface, it was possible to erase what had been written. Starting in the Middle Ages, the term referred to an altar with two hinged wings.

DISEGNO E COLORE: Beginning in late 14th-century Italy, the term *disegno* (drawing) was understood to mean an artistic idea that was usually first expressed in a (preparatory) drawing. In Lorenzo Ghiberti's *Commentarii* (ca. 1447), the term was used for the first time in connection with art theory; in 1550 Vasari used it again in the preface to his *Lives of the Most Eminent Italian Architects, Painters and Sculptors.* Vasari writes of the "tre arti del disegno" ("three types of *disegno*") and mentions painting and sculpture in addition to architecture as having their common basis in *disegno*. In contrast to this is the idea of the priority of painterly aspects (thus *colore,* Italian "colour") in realising an artistic idea, a view that was championed primarily in Venice. This was believed to be the step that gave a painting its real quality.

EMBLEM: (from Greek: *emblema,* insertion). Emblems combine word and image to illustrate ideas and convey a moral lesson. People, objects and actions are combined to create a unity with verbal commentary. Given their symbolic character, emblems are related to attributes and symbols. Andrea Alciati published the first book of emblems in Augsburg in 1532, the *Emblematum liber.* The use of emblems was especially popular between 1530 and 1650.

GENIUS: (from Latin: *gignere,* to beget). In Roman mythology, the genius embodied the reproductive power of a man. Originally each man venerated his own guardian spirit, offering sacrifices of food and incense. The woman's counterpart to the male genius was the goddess Juno as the epitome of female reproductive power. Later the genii were considered the guardian spirits of the family in general, the home or a particular place ("genius loci"). In antiquity they were initially depicted in the form of a snake or a bearded, armoured man with horn of plenty and sceptre, later generally as winged creatures of light, sometimes bearing portrait medallions and plaques with inscriptions.

GENRE PAINTING: (French: *genre,* sort, kind, type). The term genre painting did not come into common use until the 18th century, but in the terminology of art history it also applies to older works depicting scenes of everyday life. These realistic pictures, often in a small format, are not based on religious, mythological or historical events. Genre paintings were known in antiquity, for example, in Egyptian mural paintings and on Greek vases. The depiction of everyday scenes also occurs in paintings of the late Middle Ages, but it did not develop into an independent type until the 16th and 17th centuries. The height of genre painting is found in Netherlandish and Dutch art.

HABIT: (from Latin: *habitus,* attire). The apparel of members of a Roman Catholic religious order. A habit consists of individual pieces of attire that vary depending on the order.

HISTORY PAINTING: In the extended sense, the depiction of historical events, which are often enriched with legends as well as themes from religious history and mythology. Often the narration of historical events is combined with the glorification of a ruler, Early forms of history painting are found in Egyptian but especially in Greek and Roman art (e.g. the Alexander the Great mosaic in Pompeii). In the Renaissance, history painting was a fixed part of the repertoire both north and south of the Alps. Early Renaissance art theory considered the convincing portrayal of human actions and passions to be painting's highest goal, and into the 19th century, history painting enjoyed the highest significance among the academic genres of painting.

HOLY KINSHIP: According to the trinubium theory (first documented in Western theology in the 9th century), the Virgin Mary's mother, St. Anne, was married three times. After the death of Mary's father, Joachim, Anne married first Cleophas and then Salome. A daughter resulted from each of these marriages: Mary Cleophas and Mary Salome. The two daughters married in turn and had children of their own. Later the parents of St. Anne and her sister Esmeria were included in the family (the latter was the grandmother of John the Baptist). In all, Mary's extended family included 26 people from four generations. The ancient legend gained additional popularity in 1408 when the blessed Colette Boilet had a vision of the Holy Kinship. In the 15th and 16th centuries the Virgin's family became a popular subject in painting, promoted by the growing interest of the nobility in the history of their families and thus in genealogical studies.

ICONOGRAPHY: (from Greek: *eikonographia,* sketch, description). An area of art history that first involves descriptive study of a picture in order to identify, in a second step, the persons, objects and scenes depicted in it. Iconology takes this one step further by seeking encoded messages and incorporated aspects of (cultural) history and by interpreting not only the individual work but also placing it, if applicable, in a wider context. Thus it may involve the interpretation of the entire artistic decoration of a church's interior, of everything portrayed on a cabinet or of an entire cycle of graphic works.

INTERIOR: (from Old Latin: *interus,* inward, on the inside). The term refers to a picture that depicts an inside space but also applies to an entire genre. While depictions of interiors are found in late Medieval painting, they came into their own as an independent genre in the Dutch painting of the 17th century.

PAINTERLY: Used in the aesthetic sense of art scholarship, this is the opposite of "graphic". The surface of the picture is dominated not by hard contours but by soft areas of colour that flow together.

PASTORALE: (Italian: of herdsmen). An idealised depiction of a shepherd's life in an arcadian landscape. This motif, which is found in the literature of antiquity and later in the plastic arts, met the desire of the courtier or urban resident for the mythical Golden Age of simplicity, harmony and the happiness of love. Renaissance painters (especially in Venice) once again took up the motif, which had largely been neglected during the Middle Ages. The pastorale reached its peak in imitating the pastoral plays that were so popular with the nobility in the Baroque and Rococo periods *(fêtes galantes).*

PASTOSE: (from Italian: *pastoso,* doughy, soft). A term in oil painting that refers to covering or filling the surface thickly with paint. The painting is not uniformly smooth but has relief-like highs and lows.

PREDELLA: (Italian: stool, step of an altar). A painted or carved step or platform on which a winged altar is placed. Often it is also a place where relics are kept.

REPOUSSOIR: (French: foil, something that serves as a contrast to something else). Persons or objects placed in the foreground of a picture in order to heighten the effect of depth. In order not to distract the viewer from the real motif, repoussoir figures are often depicted with their backs turned. The illusion of space can be further heightened with the placement of dark draperies, furniture or shadows in the foreground, with the more brightly lit subject extending into the background.

TEMPERA PAINTING: (Italian: *tempera,* from Latin *temperare,* to temper). This technique of mixing dry pigments with a water-soluble medium to the desired consistency has been used since the earliest days of painting. The paint is mixed from inorganic pigments and a binding vehicle made from an oil, gum or wax (linseed oil, linseed-oil varnish, poppy-seed oil or nut oil) and a watery component (egg, glue, gum arabic, starch). With a sufficiently high proportion of oil or gum, tempera paint can be used in a manner similar to oil-based paint. If the watery components dominate, it can be used with water, like gouache paint. In the 15th century oil painting began to displace tempera painting, first in the Netherlands and later in Italy, but there are also mixed techniques. Compared with oil-based paints, tempera colours are far more difficult to combine with one another; they tend to separate and make the paintings appear harder. Because tempera dries quickly, it can soon be over-painted, making tempera paints suitable for base coats. In contrast to oil-based paints, tempera changes appearance as it dries, leaving a matt finish. A final varnish can heighten the luminescence, thus lessening the difference between tempera and oil paintings.

TRIPTYCH: (Greek: *triptychos*, having three folds). A painting or relief in three parts, the triptych is the most frequent form of winged altar, consisting of a central panel and two moveable side panels that are half so wide as the central one. When they are closed, the wings cover the main central part – a painted or carved panel. The exterior sides of the two wings when closed are the "everyday side": when the wings are opened the viewer sees the far more magnificent "feast-day side".

VANITAS: (Latin: quality of being empty or vain). Painters are particularly fond of using the form of the still life to convey the idea of the transitoriness of life. These paintings proclaim the ephemerality of earthly possessions, secular power and the beauty of youth against the background of an Old Testament admonition (Vanitas vanitatum, omnia vanitas [Vanity of vanities; all is vanity], Ecclesiastes 1:2). The preferred symbols are a death's head, hour-glass, mirror, extinguished candle, books, wilted flowers and withered fruit. Other devices for depicting vanitas are the dance of death and the comparison of a young and an old woman's bodies. The theme became very popular in the 16th and 17th centuries. Although there are also isolated examples in areas of Catholic influence, the admonition to avoid vanity and the reference to transitoriness were a theme preferred by Protestant artists.

VEDUTA: (Italian: view). A collective term for topographically exact (city) views. This type is mostly found in the late 17th and early 18th centuries. Views of Venice (especially those by Canaletto and Guardi), Rome and Naples were initially the most popular. Canaletto's nephew Bellotto introduced *veduta* painting to northern Europe as well, working in Dresden, Vienna, Munich and Warsaw. Artistic aspects (composition and coloration) are often only apparently subordinate to a realistic depiction of architecture, people and landscapes: the pictures combine various perspectives, and building complexes are visually unified. A special case is the *veduta ideata*, which connected existing architecture of varied provenance or completely imaginary elements in a unified view.

GENERAL INTRODUCTION TO ART HISTORY: A SELECTION

E. H. Gombrich, *The Story of Art,* 16th ed., New York 1995

The Oxford History of Western Art, edited by M. Kemp, Oxford 2000

H. Honour – J. Fleming, *The Visual Arts: A History,* 6th ed., New York 2002

P. de Rynck, *How to Read a Painting: Decoding, Understanding and Enjoying the Old Masters,* London 2004

Janson's History of Art: Western Tradition, 7th ed., New York 2006

GUIDES AND CATALOGUES OF HOLDINGS

[E. Ritter von Engerth], *Kunsthistorische Sammlungen des Allerhöchsten Kaiserhauses. Gemälde. Beschreibendes Verzeichnis,* Vol. I–III, Vienna 1882, 2th ed. Vienna 1884

Die Gemäldegalerie des Kunsthistorischen Museums in Wien, edited by G. Glück, Vienna 1925

E. H. Buschbeck, *Kunsthistorisches Museum Wien. Führer durch die Gemäldegalerie,* Vienna 1928

V. Oberhammer, *Die Gemäldegalerie des Kunsthistorischen Museums in Wien,* 2 Vols., Vienna – Munich 1959

LITERATURE

[G. Heinz – F. Klauner], *Katalog der Gemäldegalerie. I. Teil: Italiener, Spanier, Franzosen, Engländer,* Vienna 1960

[G. Heinz – F. Klauner], *Katalog der Gemäldegalerie. II. Teil: Vlamen, Holländer, Deutsche, Franzosen,* 2th ed. Vienna 1963

[K. Demus], *Katalog der Gemäldegalerie. Holländische Meister des 15., 16. und 17. Jahrhunderts,* Vienna 1972

F. Klauner, *Die Gemäldegalerie des Kunsthistorischen Museums in Wien. Vier Jahrhunderte europäischer Malerei,* Salzburg 1978

[K. Demus – F. Klauner – K. Schütz], *Flämische Malerei von Jan van Eyck bis Pieter Bruegel d. A.,* Vienna 1981

[K. Schütz], *Gemäldegalerie Kunsthistorisches Museum Wien* (museum), Braunschweig 1984

G. Heinz, *Das Neue Testament,* in: F. Klauner – G. Heinz, *Vom Himmel durch die Welt zur Hölle. Inhalt und Sinn von Gemälden,* Salzburg – Vienna 1987, 304 ff.

Flämische Malerei im Kunsthistorischen Museum Wien, Zurich 1989

S. Ferino-Pagden – W. Prohaska – K. Schütz, *Die Gemäldegalerie des Kunsthistorischen Museums in Wien. Verzeichnis der Gemälde,* edited by W. Seipel, Vienna 1991

Kunsthistorisches Museum. The Picture Gallery, edited by W. Seipel, Vienna 1996 (Ger., Eng., Ital., Jap.)

W. Prohaska, *Kunsthistorisches Museum Vienna: The Paintings,* in the series "Museen der Welt", 3rd ed. Munich – London 2004 (Ger., Eng., Ital., Fre., Jap., Russ.)

Kunsthistorisches Museum Vienna. Guide, 6th ed. Vienna 2005 (Ger., Eng., Ital., Jap.)

The Kunsthistorisches Museum in Vienna (Prestel Museum Guides), Munich – Berlin – London – New York 2007 (Ger., Eng., Fre., Ital.)

INDIVIDUAL ARTISTS AND CATALOGUES TO KHM EXHIBITIONS AS FROM 1990

Von Bruegel bis Rubens. Das goldene Jahrhundert der flämischen Malerei, edited by E. Mai – H. Vlieghe, Cologne – Antwerp – Vienna 1993

K. Schütz, *Albrecht Dürer im Kunsthistorischen Museum,* Vienna 1994

W. Seipel, *Bellotto. Wien vom Belvedere aus gesehen* (I capolavori dell'arte), Vienna 1996 (Ger., Ital.)

A. Wied, *Bruegel: Der Kampf zwischen Fasching und Fasten* (I capolavori dell'arte), Vienna 1996 (Ger., Ital.)

Pieter Bruegel the Elder at the KHM in Vienna, edited by W. Seipel, Vienna 1997 (Ger., Eng., Ital.)

Pieter Breughel der Jüngere – Jan Brueghel der Ältere. Flämische Malerei um 1600. Tradition und Fortschritt, edited by W. Seipel, Essen – Vienna 1998

Luca Giordano 1634–1705, edited by W. Seipel, Vienna 2001

Das flämische Stillleben, edited by W. Seipel, Vienna 2002

Die flämische Landschaft 1520–1700, edited by W. Seipel, Vienna 2003

Parmigianino und der europäische Manierismus, edited by S. Ferino-Pagden – L. Fornari Schianchi, Vienna 2003

Giorgione. Mythos und Enigma, edited by S. Ferino-Pagden – G. Nepi Scirè, Vienna 2004

Rubens in Vienna. The Masterpieces, edited by J. Kräftner – R. Trnek – W. Seipel, Vienna 2004

Bernardo Bellotto gen. Canaletto. Europäische Veduten, edited by W. Seipel, Vienna 2005

Bellini, Giorgione, Tizian und die Renaissance der venezianischen Malerei, Vienna 2006

Der späte Tizian und die Sinnlichkeit in der Malerei (Late Titian and the Sensuousness of Painting), with English Translation, Vienna 2007

Rom in Wien. Angelo Carosellis Bilder im KHM, Vienna 2007

Arcimboldo 1526–1593, Vienna 2007 (Ger., Eng., Fre., Ital.)

Additionen. Neuerwerbungen des Kunsthistorischen Museums 1990–2008, Vienna 2008

Vom Mythos der Antike, edited by W. Seipel, Vienna 2008

Gudrun Swoboda, *Die Wege der Bilder. Eine Geschichte der kaiserlichen Gemäldesammlungen von 1600 bis 1800,* Vienna 2008

Karl Schütz, *Raum im Bild. Interieurmalerei 1500 bis 1900,* edited by S. Haag, Vienna 2009

Vermeer. Die Malkunst, edited by S. Haag, E. Oberthaler and S. Pénot, Vienna 2010

Starke Köpfe. Porträt(s) des Kunsthistorischen Museums, edited by S. Haag, Vienna 2010

INDEX OF WORKS AND THEIR PROVENANCE

CAT. NO.	INV. NO.	ARTIST	TITLE	PROVENANCE
1	975	Jan van Eyck	Cardinal Niccolò Albergati	acquired in 1648 by Archduke Leopold Wilhelm
2	901	Rogier van der Weyden	Triptych: The Crucifixion	1659 Archduke Leopold Wilhelm
3	301	Andrea Mantegna	St. Sebastian	1659 Archduke Leopold Wilhelm
4	5822 A, 945	Hugo van der Goes	The Fall of Man and The Lamentation	1659 Archduke Leopold Wilhelm
5	2574	Antonello da Messina	Madonna with the Saints Nicholas of Bari, Anastasia, Ursula and Dominic	1659 Archduke Leopold Wilhelm
6	843	Martin Schongauer	The Holy Family	acquired in 1865
7	993	Geertgen tot Sint Jans	Legend of the Relics of St. John the Baptist	1659 Archduke Leopold Wilhelm
8	939, 943 a, b	Hans Memling	Small Triptych of St. John the Baptist	1659 Archduke Leopold Wilhelm
9	6905	Lucas Cranach the Elder	The Crucifixion	acquired in 1934
10	111	Giorgione	Three Philosophers	1659 Archduke Leopold Wilhelm
11	6440	Albrecht Dürer	Portrait of a Young Venetian Woman	acquired in 1923
12	175	Raphael	Madonna in the Meadow	acquired in 1662 by Archduke Ferdinand Karl
13	31	Giorgione	Young Woman ("Laura")	1659 Archduke Leopold Wilhelm
14	95	Titian	Gipsy Madonna	1659 Archduke Leopold Wilhelm
15	838	Albrecht Dürer	Adoration of the Trinity (Landauer Altar)	acquired in 1585 by Emperor Rudolf II
16	992	Bernaerd van Orley	Altarpiece of Saints Thomas and Matthias	acquired in 1809
17	182	Andrea del Sarto	The Archangel Raphael with Tobias, St. Leonard and the Donor, Leonardo di Lorenzo Morelli	acquired in 1792 in an exchange between Florence and Vienna
18	848	Albrecht Dürer	Virgin and Child with a Pear	acquired in 1600 by Emperor Rudolf II (?)
19	63	Palma il Vecchio	Young Woman in a Blue Dress, with Fan	1659 Archduke Leopold Wilhelm
20	981	Joachim Patinier	The Baptism of Christ	1659 Archduke Leopold Wilhelm
21	97	Giovanni Bellini	Young Woman at Her Toilette	1659 Archduke Leopold Wilhelm
22	207	Fra Bartolomeo	The Scene of Christ in the Temple	acquired in 1792 in an exchange between Florence and Vienna
23	832	Bernhard Strigel	Emperor Maximilian I with His Family	early holding; documented in the imperial portrait collection in Vienna before 1600
24	6796	Albrecht Altdorfer	The Resurrection of Christ	acquired in 1930 from St. Florian Abbey

CAT. NO.	INV. NO.	ARTIST	TITLE	PROVENANCE
25	825	Albrecht Dürer	Portrait of Maximilian I	early imperial possession
26	894	Jan Gossaert	St. Luke Painting the Madonna	1659 Archduke Leopold Wilhelm
27	286	Parmigianino	Self-Portrait in a Convex Mirror	1608 collection of Emperor Rudolf II
28	850	Albrecht Dürer	Johannes Kleberger	acquired in 1588 by Emperor Rudolf II
29	101	Lorenzo Lotto	Madonna and Child with Saints Catherine and Thomas (sacra conversazione)	in imperial possession in 1660
30	61	Moretto da Brescia	St. Justina, Venerated by a Patron	1663 Ambras Collection
31	274	Correggio	Jupiter and Io	acquired in 1601 by Emperor Rudolf II
32	276	Correggio	The Abduction of Ganymede	acquired in 1603 by Emperor Rudolf II
33	858	Lucas Cranach the Elder	Judith with the Head of Holofernes	1612/18 Vienna Inventory G
34	275	Parmigianino	Bow-carving Amor	1603 art collection of Emperor Rudolf II
35	89	Titian	Girl in a Fur	acquired in 1651
36	881	Hans Holbein the Younger	Jane Seymour, Queen of England	documented in the gallery since 1720
37	990	Maerten van Heemskerck	The Triumphal Procession of Bacchus	1659 Archduke Leopold Wilhelm
38	73	Titian	Ecce Homo	acquired in 1649
39	183	Bronzino	Holy Family with St. Anne and the Infant St. John	from Florence to Vienna as an exchange in 1792
40	6927	Pieter Aertsen	Christ with Mary and Martha	1659 Archduke Leopold Wilhelm
41	78	Giovanni Baptista Moroni	The Sculptor Alessandro Vittoria	1659 Archduke Leopold Wilhelm
42	308	Tintoretto	Lorenzo Soranzo	in the gallery in 1824
43	361	Jacopo Bassano	Adoration of the Magi	1659 Archduke Leopold Wilhelm
44	40	Paolo Veronese	The Anointment of David	acquired in 1649
45	1530	Tintoretto	Susanna and the Elders	in the gallery before 1712
46	1017	Pieter Bruegel the Elder	Children's Games	acquired in 1594 by Archduke Ernst in Brussels
47	1589	Giuseppe Arcimboldo	Summer	from the art collection of Emperor Rudolf II
48	1026	Pieter Bruegel the Elder	The Tower of Babel	a possession of Emperor Rudolf II
49	3235	Alonso Sánchez Coello	Infant Don Carlos of Spain	acquired in 1564
50	1838	Pieter Bruegel the Elder	Hunters in the Snow (Winter)	1595 estate of Archduke Ernst
51	81	Titian	Jacopo Strada	1659 Archduke Leopold Wilhelm

CAT. NO.	INV. NO.	ARTIST	TITLE	PROVENANCE
52	1027	Pieter Bruegel the Elder	Peasant Wedding	acquired in 1594 by Archduke Ernst in Brussels
53	1825	Titian	Nymph and Shepherd	1659 Archduke Leopold Wilhelm
54	25	Tintoretto	Man with a White Beard	1659 Archduke Leopold Wilhelm
55	2613	Bartholomäus Spranger	Hercules, Deianira and the Centaur Nessus	from the art collection of Emperor Rudolf II
56	34	Paolo Veronese	Judith with the Head of Holofernes	1659 Archduke Leopold Wilhelm
57	1098	Hans von Aachen	Bacchus, Ceres and Amor (?)	1621 Prague Inventory
58	147	Caravaggio	Madonna of the Rosary	a gift to Emperor Joseph II in 1781
59	307	Caravaggio	The Crowning with Thorns	acquired in 1810 in Rome
60	570	Jan Brueghel the Elder	Flowers in a Wooden Vessel	1659 Archduke Leopold Wilhelm
61	F 17	Giovanni Battista Caracciolo	Christ on the Mount of Olives	1659 Archduke Leopold Wilhelm
62	528	Peter Paul Rubens	The Miracles of St. Francis Xavier, *modello*	acquired in 1776 from the professed house of the Jesuits in Antwerp
63	519	Peter Paul Rubens	The Miracles of St. Francis Xavier	acquired in 1776 from the Jesuit Church in Antwerp
64	160	Domenico Fetti	Hero Mourning the Dead Leander	1659 Archduke Leopold Wilhelm
65	222	Guido Reni	The Baptism of Christ	acquired in 1649
66	690	Peter Paul Rubens	Landscape with Philemon and Baucis	1659 Archduke Leopold Wilhelm
67	501	Anton van Dyck	Nicolas Lanier	documented in the gallery since 1720
68	488	Anton van Dyck	The Vision of the Blessed Hermann Joseph	acquired in 1776 from the Jesuit congregation in Antwerp
69	512	Anton van Dyck	Samson and Delilah	1659 Archduke Leopold Wilhelm
70	678	Peter Paul Rubens	The Triptych of St. Ildefonso	acquired in 1777 from Coudenberg Abbey
71	771	Antonio de Pereda	Allegory of Vanity	documented in the gallery since 1733
72	684	Peter Paul Rubens	The Feast of Venus	1685 Prague Inventory
73	688	Peter Paul Rubens	Helena Fourment in a Fur Robe	documented in the gallery since 1730
74	1556	Nicolas Poussin	The Conquest of Jerusalem by Emperor Titus	1685 Prague Inventory
75	527	Peter Paul Rubens	Self-Portrait	documented in the gallery since 1720
76	6764	Bernardo Cavallino	Adoration of the Magi	acquired in 1928

CAT. NO.	INV. NO.	ARTIST	TITLE	PROVENANCE
77	599	Wolfgang Heimbach	Banquet at Night	documented in the gallery since 1772
78	413	Leonaert Bramer	Allegory of Vanity (Vanitas)	acquired between 1772 and 1781 from the Abbey of the Scots in Vienna
79	786	Jacob Jordaens	The Feast of the Bean King	1659 Archduke Leopold Wilhelm
80	256	Bernardo Strozzi	The Sermon of St. John the Baptist	1685 Prague Inventory
81	739	David Teniers the Younger	Archduke Leopold William in his Gallery at Brussels	painted for Archduke Leopold Wilhelm
82	411	Rembrandt	Large Self-Portrait	documented in the gallery since 1720
83	426	Jacob van Ruisdael	The Great Forest	acquired in 1806
84	410	Rembrandt	Titus van Rijn, the Artist's Son, Reading	documented in the gallery since 1720
85	2130	Diego Velázquez	Infanta Margarita Teresa in a Blue Dress	a gift to the Vienna court in 1659
86	260	Guido Cagnacci	The Death of Cleopatra	1659 Archduke Leopold Wilhelm
87	586	Frans van Mieris the Elder	Cavalier in the Shop	1659 Archduke Leopold Wilhelm
88	791	Jan Steen	Beware of Luxury ("In Weelde Siet Toe")	acquired in 1780
89	5976	Pieter de Hooch	Woman and Child with Serving Maid	Goldschmidt gift in 1903
90	9128	Johannes Vermeer	The Art of Painting	acquired in 1946
91	350	Luca Giordano	The Fall of the Rebel Angels	documented in the gallery since 1796
92	1601	Francesco Solimena	Emperor Charles VI and Count Gundacker Althann	came to Vienna in 1728
93	3507	Francesco Solimena	The Deposition	acquired in 1752
94	6271	Thomas Gainsborough	Landscape in Suffolk	acquired in 1913
95	1669	Bernardo Bellotto	Vienna Viewed from the Belvedere Palace	since its creation in imperial possession
96	1672	Bernardo Bellotto	Vienna, Dominican Church	since its creation in imperial possession
97	1628	Pompeo Batoni	Emperor Joseph II with Grand Duke Pietro Leopoldo of Tuscany	in the imperial gallery in 1824
98	124	Anton Raphael Mengs	The Dream of St. Joseph	in the imperial gallery in 1796
99	1795	Joseph Siffred Duplessis	Christoph Willibald Gluck	in the imperial gallery in 1824
100	6234	Francesco Guardi	The Entrance to the Arsenal in Venice	acquired in 1912

INDEX OF IVENTORY AND CATALOGUE NUMBERS

INVENTORY NUMBER	CATALOGUE NUMBER	INVENTORY NUMBER	CATALOGUE NUMBER	INVENTORY NUMBER	CATALOGUE NUMBER
25	54	411	82	981	20
31	13	413	78	990	37
34	56	426	83	992	16
40	44	488	68	993	7
61	30	501	67	1017	46
63	19	512	69	1026	48
73	38	519	63	1027	52
78	41	527	75	1098	57
81	51	528	62	1530	45
89	35	570	60	1556	74
95	14	586	87	1589	47
97	21	599	77	1601	92
101	29	678	70	1628	97
111	10	684	72	1669	95
124	98	688	73	1672	96
147	58	690	66	1795	99
160	64	739	81	1825	53
175	12	771	71	1838	50
182	17	786	79	2130	85
183	39	791	88	2574	5
207	22	825	25	2613	55
222	65	832	23	3235	49
256	80	838	15	3507	93
260	86	843	6	5822 A	4
274	31	848	18	5976	89
275	34	850	28	6234	100
276	32	858	33	6271	94
286	27	881	36	6440	11
301	3	894	26	6764	76
307	59	901	2	6796	24
308	42	939	8	6905	9
350	91	943 a, b	8	6927	40
361	43	945	4	9128	90
410	84	975	1	F 17	61

INDEX OF ARTISTS

ARTIST	TITLE	CAT. NO.
Eyck, Jan van	Cardinal Niccolò Albergati	1
Fetti, Domenico	Hero Mourning the Dead Leander	64
Fra Bartolomeo	The Scene of Christ in the Temple	22
Gainsborough, Thomas	Landscape in Suffolk	94
Geertgen tot Sint Jans	Legend of the Relics of St. John the Baptist	7
Giordano, Luca	The Fall of the Rebel Angels	91
Giorgione	Three Philosophers	10
Giorgione	Young Woman ("Laura")	13
Goes, Hugo van der	The Fall of Man and The Lamentation	4
Gossaert, Jan	St. Luke Painting the Madonna	26
Guardi, Francesco	The Entrance to the Arsenal in Venice	100
Heemskerck, Maerten van	The Triumphal Procession of Bacchus	37
Heimbach, Wolfgang	Banquet at Night	77
Holbein the Younger, Hans	Jane Seymour, Queen of England	36
Hooch, Pieter de	Woman and Child with Serving Maid	89
Jordaens, Jacob	The Feast of the Bean King	79
Lotto, Lorenzo	Madonna and Child with Saints Catherine and Thomas	29
Mantegna, Andrea	St. Sebastian	3
Memling, Hans	Small Triptych of St. John the Baptist	8
Mengs, Anton Raphael	The Dream of St. Joseph	98
Messina, Antonello da	Madonna with the Saints Nicholas of Bari, Anastasia, Ursula and Dominic	5
Mieris the Elder, Frans van	Cavalier in the Shop	87
Moretto da Brescia	St. Justina, Venerated by a Patron	30
Moroni, Giovanni Battista	The Sculptor Alessandro Vittoria	41
Orley, Bernaerd van	Altarpiece of Saints Thomas and Matthias	16
Palma il Vecchio	Young Woman in a Blue Dress, with Fan	19
Parmigianino	Self-Portrait in a Convex Mirror	27
Parmigianino	Bow-carving Amor	34
Patinier, Joachim	The Baptism of Christ	20
Pereda, Antonio de	Allegory of Vanity	71
Poussin, Nicolas	The Conquest of Jerusalem by Emperor Titus	74
Raphael	Madonna in the Meadow	12
Rembrandt	Large Self-Portrait	82

ARTIST	TITLE	CAT. NO.
Rembrandt	Titus van Rijn, the Artist's Son, Reading	84
Reni, Guido	The Baptism of Christ	65
Rubens, Peter Paul	The Miracles of St. Francis Xavier, *modello*	62
Rubens, Peter Paul	The Miracles of St. Francis Xavier	63
Rubens, Peter Paul	Landscape with Philemon and Baucis	66
Rubens, Peter Paul	The Triptych of St. Ildefonso	70
Rubens, Peter Paul	The Feast of Venus	72
Rubens, Peter Paul	Helena Fourment in a Fur Robe	73
Rubens, Peter Paul	Self-Portrait	75
Ruisdael, Jacob van	The Great Forest	83
Sánchez Coello, Alonso	Infant Don Carlos of Spain	49
Sarto, Andrea del	The Archangel Raphael with Tobias, St. Leonard and the Donor, Leonardo di Lorenzo Morelli	17
Schongauer, Martin	The Holy Family	6
Solimena, Francesco	Emperor Charles VI and Count Gundacker Althann	92
Solimena, Francesco	The Deposition	93
Spranger, Bartholomäus	Hercules, Deianira and the Centaur Nessus	55
Steen, Jan	Beware of Luxury ("In Weelde Siet Toe")	88
Strigel, Bernhard	Emperor Maximilian I with His Family	23
Strozzi, Bernardo	The Sermon of St. John the Baptist	80
Teniers the Younger, David	Archduke Leopold William in his Gallery at Brussels	81
Tintoretto	Lorenzo Soranzo	42
Tintoretto	Susanna and the Elders	45
Tintoretto	Man with a White Beard	54
Titian	Gipsy Madonna	14
Titian	Girl in a Fur	35
Titian	Ecce Homo	38
Titian	Jacopo Strada	51
Titian	Nymph and Shepherd	53
Velázquez, Diego	Infanta Margarita Teresa in a Blue Dress	85
Vermeer, Johannes	The Art of Painting	90
Veronese, Paolo	The Anointment of David	44
Veronese, Paolo	Judith with the Head of Holofernes	56
Weyden, Rogier van der	Triptych: The Crucifixion	2